2C
Fourth Edition
Generations
KB240431
SLE
SPEAKING · LISTENING · EXPRESSION
PAGODA Books

Copyright © 2013, 2008, 2001, 1997 by **PAGODA Books**

All rights reserved. No part of this publication may be reproduced, stored in a retrieval system, or transmitted, in any form, or by any means, electronic, mechanical, photocopying, recording or otherwise, without the prior written permission of the copyright holder and the publisher.

Published by PAGODA Books
PAGODA Books is the professional language publishing company of the **PAGODA** Education Group.
19F, PAGODA Tower, 419, Gangnam-daero,
Seocho-gu, Seoul, 06614, Rep. of KOREA
www.pagodabook.com

First published 2013
Twelfth impression 2023
Printed in the Republic of Korea

ISBN 978-89-6281-455-2 (13740)

Publisher | Kyung-Sil Park
Writers | Judson Wright, Lee Robinson, Kristin Quackenbush
Editor | Paul Adams
Advisor | Ruda Go
Illustrator | Dae Ho Kim

Acknowledgements
Sang Hee Kang, Song Rim Park, Hana Sakuragi, Stephen Willetts, Ian Windsor, and Gemma Young for their support
Chasity Davis, Christina DeMers, Mike Dent, Martin Middleton, Tiara Smith, and Meredith Watson for trialing and feedback
Rich Debourke, Jay Hilalen, Jess Kroll, and Tiara Smith for voice recording.

A defective book may be exchanged at the store where you purchased it.

To Our Students

The SLE program is a conversation program for adult and young adult students who want to improve their English in an enjoyable, effective, and authentic way. The book allows students to use English in a variety of contexts with an emphasis on different useful functions. Our goal is to improve your confidence in your speaking, listening, reading, and writing ability while improving your vocabulary and grammar skills. We will help you to understand not only the "How" but the "Why" of English usage.

The SLE Level 2 textbook series is meant for students with a very good understanding of the basics of English.
The material in this book focuses on building students' ability to perform basic functions and use essential structures.

Contents SLE 2C

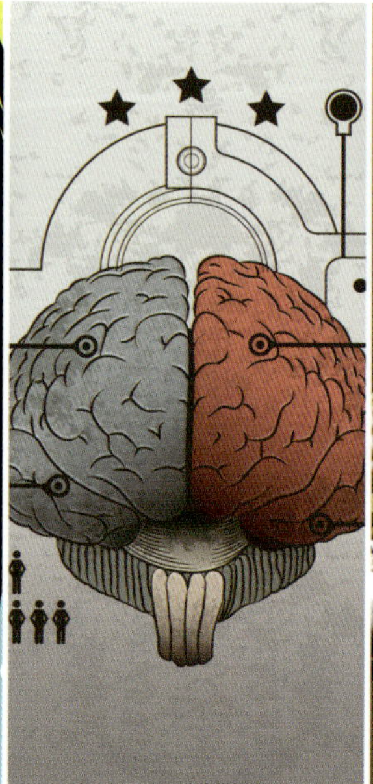

Format of the Book:

Overall Format >

There are ten units in this textbook, each with its own focus. In each unit there are two individual lessons. The focus of the lesson is either grammatical or topical. Each unit consists of the following elements:

Warm Up >

The warm up for each lesson has its own purpose. The lesson one warm up is used as an opportunity to start thinking about the topic and includes functional language such as idioms, collocations, and tongue twisters that relate to the topic as a whole. The lesson two warm up is used as a quick review of the language used in the first lesson and a bridge to the second lesson.

WARM UP

Ask your partner a question.
up question, and think of ano
conversation going.
1. What was the last
(Movie/Play/Art Show/Co
How was it?

Listening >

Each listening follows the story of the Thompson family and relates to the unit topic and language points used in that unit. Each listening requires the student to make predictions based on illustrations and use communicative language to discuss what they have heard.

Listening 

Richard is trying to make plans with his indecisive high school classmate, Stan.
While you're listening, check the person, place, or thing Richard and his friend decide on.

Language Point >

Language points occur at the start of any activity where a specific grammar or function point is used in that activity and needs to be explained to the student.

A. The Devil's Debate

Choose one of the opinions below, and simply say whethe
you agree or disagree. Your partner(s) MUST disagree with

Example: It is acceptable for both men and women to stay at home a
A: *I believe that it is perfectly acceptable for men to stay at home*
B: *I disagree. Even if a man is good with children it is really important that a mothe or she is young.*

1. It is equally acceptable for men and wo to stay home and take care of c

Activities >

Each lesson consists of a structured activity, a communicative activity, and a task based activity. All units include a "Bonus activity" that can add to the lesson.

Discussion Questions >

Each lesson has a short series of discussion questions that relate to the topic and encourage the use of asking follow up questions.

Discussion Questions

1 What is your favorite mo
▶ What is it that you
Who are some of

Boxes >

Several boxes are found throughout the text and have different functions:

- **Recycle Box**
  Reminds the student of language points they have used previously in SLE.
- **Third Wheel**
  Gives a suggestion of how students can perform an activity with an extra student.
- **Do You Know?**
  Explains the reason why language is used in a specific way.
- **Do You Remember?**
  Reminds students of vocabulary from a previous lesson.
- **Tip**
  Gives a tip on how the student can acquire the language easier.

Segue Activity >

The segue activity consists of a reading that relates to the topic of the listening, discussion questions which check the comprehension of the reading, and a short writing task on the topic.

Goals for the Course:

1
You should be able to use the following grammatical structures:

- **a** Expressing strength of opinion with "for" and "to"
- **b** "-ever" words
- **c** "Be supposed to" and "be expected to"
- **d** "Even if," "only if," and "unless"
- **e** Adjective order
- **f** Using the verb "wish"
- **g** Gerunds when defining concepts

2
You should be able to perform the following functions:

- **a** Describing and defining abstract concepts
- **b** Raising considerations
- **c** Negotiating and compromising
- **d** Describing responsibilities and expectations
- **e** Stipulating conditions
- **f** Discussing resolutions for complex problems
- **g** Using euphemism, exaggeration, and sentence stress
- **h** Expressing skepticism
- **i** Making inferences to fill in missing information

Need to Know:

- **to be fired**
  Lucas **was fired** from his job because he stole money from the safe.
- **to be laid off**
  Because of budget cuts, thirty employees **were laid off** last week.
- **to retire**
  My parents **retired** when they were 60 years old.
- **to quit**
  She **quit** her job because the salary was too low.
- **to get promoted**
  When Fred **got promoted**, he received a higher salary.

Meet the Thompson Family

Several of the activities will follow their lives and daily routines.

Jack Thompson

Age: 22
Blood type: A
Job: Senior at University

Jack is a friendly, relaxed young man, though many people think he is very lazy. He enjoys drinking with his friends and listening to his favorite band: the Crimson Kings. He will graduate from university soon and is starting to look for a new job. But not very hard.

Susan Thompson

Age: 42
Blood type: B
Job: Owns a small catering business

Susan is a logical, smart, and independent woman. She loves reading non-fiction, especially biographies. In her free time, Susan enjoys relaxing with an old movie and a large cup of tea.

Baby Jane

Charles Thompson

Age: 67
Blood type: O
Job: Retired

Richard's Father. Charles is an adventurous old man with the heart of a child. He doesn't always consider the consequences of his actions. When he was younger, he joined the military and traveled the world. He enjoys hiking and fishing.

Richard Thompson

Age: 45
Blood type: A
Job: Marketing

Richard is a motivated, hard-working, and creative man. He enjoys spending time with his family. He is an excellent cook. He also reads lots of different newspapers. He is very good at his job, and he recently received a new promotion.

Martha Thompson

Age: 65
Blood type: A
Job: Retired

Richard's Mother. Martha is a kind and quirky old woman, though sometimes she is a little forgetful. She writes poetry and secretly loves watching reality television. She is very concerned about eating healthy food.

Mr. Squiggles

Age: 3
Job: Cat

Mr. Squiggles is the playful family cat. He enjoys eating, scratching furniture, taking naps in Lisa's lap, and chasing Jack around the house. Sometimes, he likes to take Susan's things and hide them under the couch.

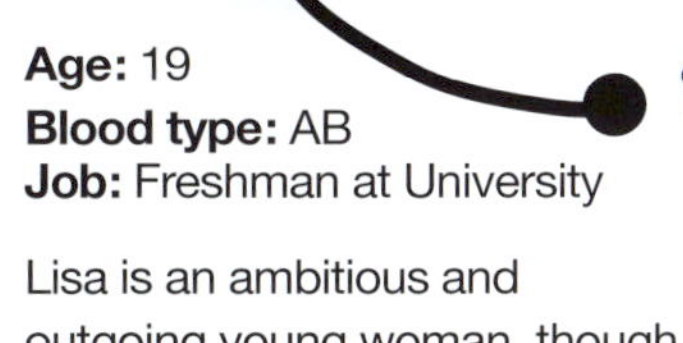

Lisa Thompson

Age: 19
Blood type: AB
Job: Freshman at University

Lisa is an ambitious and outgoing young woman, though her ambition sometimes means she gets easily stressed. She graduated high school last year and this is her first year of university. She loves going to the park on sunny days and shopping on rainy days.

Humm...
Are You
Ready To Meet
Them?

01

Self Portraits

Art and Media

Objectives:

/ Discuss various forms of art and media
/ Listen to a conversation about the pieces at an art show

WARM UP

Ask your partner a question. Then, ask a follow up question, and think of another to keep the conversation going.

1. What was the last ____________________ you saw?

(Movie/Play/Art Show/Concert)

- How was it?

2. Who is your favorite singer or band?

- What is their best album?
- Have you ever seen them live?

IDIOMS

- **A piece**
  I painted this *piece* when I was in University.
- **Catch a flick**
  I'm bored. Do you want to go *catch a flick*?

PHRASAL VERBS

- **Check out**
  You should *check out* the new exhibit at the Museum of Modern Art. It's really interesting!
- **Get into**
  I really *got into* their music when I was in university.

COLLOCATIONS

- **Get it**
  I went with my girlfriend to this art performance. It seemed interesting, but I didn't really *get it*.
- **Good/Bad Taste**
  She has really *good taste* in music. Every time she recommends something, I like it.

LESSON 1

A. You Are How You Live

The way we live, as well as the design of the things we own, gives other people an idea of who we are.
In each category, choose one object to add to your home and explain how it represents you. Think of adjectives that describe each object.

Example:

I think that a wood cabin with solar panels represents me because I am both outdoorsy and I care about the environment..

Your House

☐ House

☐ **Igloo**

☐ Castle

☐ Wood Cabin with Solar Panels

☐ Upside-down House

Your Car

☐ Electric Car

☐ Bulldozer

☐ Race Car

☐ **Camper**

☐ Classic Car

Camper ***(n.)*****:** self-contained traveling home
Igloo ***(n.)*****:** dome-shaped building built from blocks of snow

A Statue in Front of Your House

☐ Religious

☐ **Abstract**

☐ Tribal

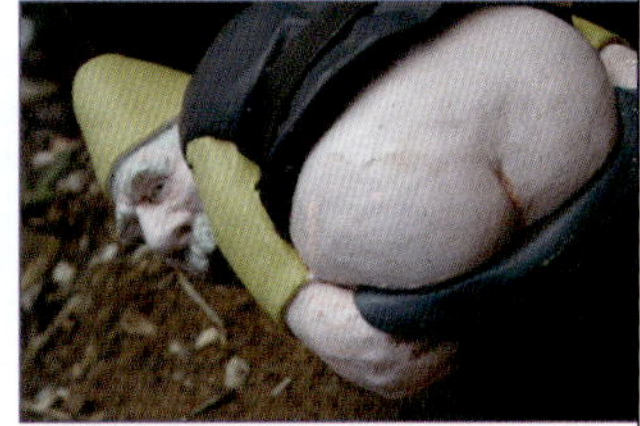
☐ Humorous

Your Furniture

☐ Contemporary

☐ Victorian

☐ Retro

Your Bookshelf

☐ Old Books

☐ **Bestselling** Books

☐ Comic Books

☐ Text Books

☐ eBooks

On the Stereo

☐ Hip Hop

☐ Jazz

☐ Pop

☐ Talk Radio

☐ Classical

In the Kitchen

☐ Chicken & Waffles

☐ Wine & Cheese

☐ Sushi

☐ Homemade Soup

Abstract (*adj.*): not depicting an object, just form
Bestselling (*adj.*): bought by many

B. Art Show, Smart Show

Pre-listening

How would you describe each of the paintings below?

- What adjectives from the list below would you use for each one?

Listening TRACK 2-3

Which three **pieces** do Grandma Martha and Lisa discuss at the student art show?

C

E

D

Post-listening

1. Grandma said that she didn't "get" the last image that Lisa liked. Do you get the image? What do you think about it?

2. Do you agree with Lisa and Martha's descriptions of the art pieces? Why or why not?
   - Which piece is your favorite?

Deep (*adj.*): Extremely intellectual
Original (*adj.*): creative
Piece (*n.*): a single artistic work
Pretentious (*adj.*): made to look important
Subtle (*adj.*): cleverly indirect

C. But Is It Art?

Look at the objects and pictures:

- What adjectives would you use to describe each piece? Give the piece a title!
- Which of these pieces in your opinion are art? Which are not?
- Think back to your house from Activity A. Which of these pieces would you use to decorate the house?
- Rank the images in order from most impressive to least impressive, and explain your choices.

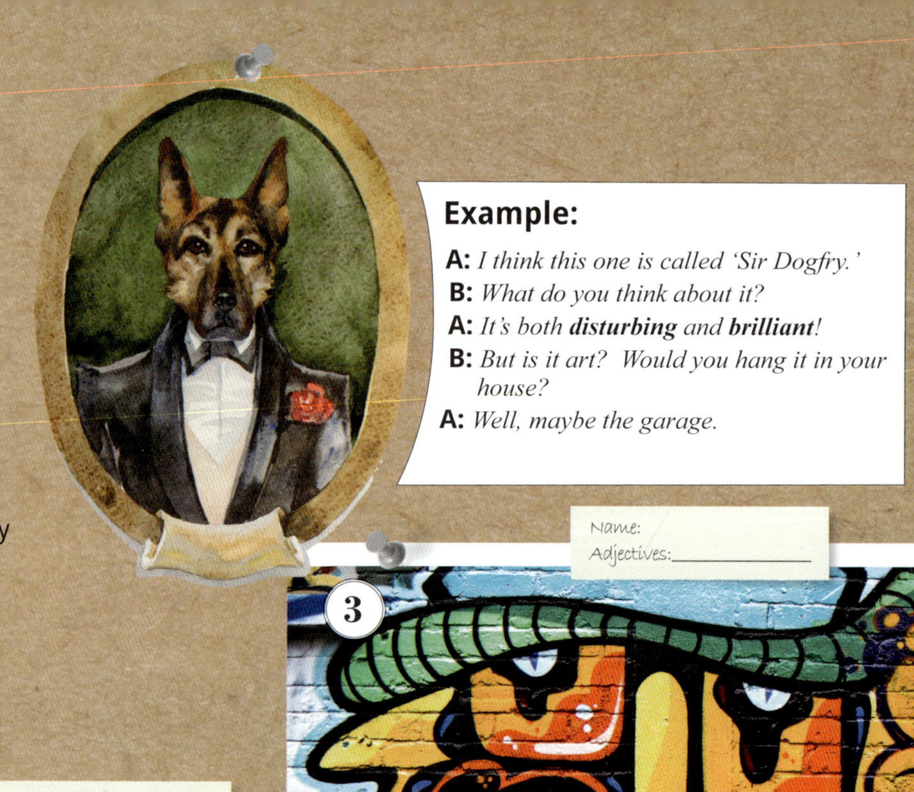

Example:

A: *I think this one is called 'Sir Dogfry.'*
B: *What do you think about it?*
A: *It's both **disturbing** and **brilliant**!*
B: *But is it art? Would you hang it in your house?*
A: *Well, maybe the garage.*

1 
Name:
Adjectives:________

2 
Name:
Adjectives:________

3 
Name:
Adjectives:________

4 
Name:
Adjectives:________

5 
Name:
Adjectives:________

6 
Name:
Adjectives:________

7 
Name:
Adjectives:________

8 
Name:
Adjectives:________

9 
Name:
Adjectives:________

Discussion Questions

1 Do you think that people are born with artistic talent or is it something that is learned?

2 Would you consider yourself to be artistic?

- What kind of art do you like to create?
- If you don't like creating art, what kinds of art do you appreciate?

3 Some people think that tattoos are a form of art. What do you think?

4 In your opinion what is an amazing **piece** in terms of…

- …Product design?
- …Architecture?
- …Food?
- …Performance?

5 Do you think you have **good taste** in products such as furniture, clothing, cars, books, etc.?

6 What kind of books do you like to read?

- Have you ever tried to read a book that you found really hard to get into and given up?

7 Where is the best place to see art where you live?

Good/bad taste *(idiom)*: ability to judge
piece *(n.)*: a single artistic work

LESSON 2

Objectives:

/ Use for and to when expressing strength of opinions

>> WARM UP

Compare the genres in each category.
Which is better?
Why do you think so?

MUSIC

DJ

Opera

DANCE

Ballet

Hip hop

LITERATURE

Magazine

Book

ARCHITECTURE

Classic

Modern

A. Portrait of an Artist

Language Point : Strength of Opinion Using For and To

It's not important **to**...	It's important **to**...	It's necessary **to**...

...study art. ("**to** do something" is used for general statements)

It's not important **for**...	It's important **for**...	It's necessary **for**...

...an artist **to** go to art school. (**for** a specific person or thing **to** do/be)

PART 1 ● Agree or disagree with the following opinions on the Arts. Give a reason why you feel that way.

1. It's important for design to have a purpose.
   Do you agree or disagree? Why?

2. It's sort of important for students to study art.
   Do you agree or disagree? Why?

3. It's actually not necessary for musicians to get money from downloaded songs.
   Do you agree or disagree? Why?

4. It's really important for a film to have not only great effects, but also an engaging story and good actors.
   Do you agree or disagree? Why?

Tip

Native speakers often use adverbs such as: *really*, *very*, and *absolutely* to add emphasis to opinions.

Example: *It's **really** not necessary to have a lot of knowledge to appreciate art.*

DJ ***(n.)***: somebody who plays recorded music

PART 2 ● Look at the various types of artists below. What is necessary for them to be successful? What isn't important?

Example:

A: *It's important for a DJ to have great musical taste and a good ear.*

B: *That's true. It's unnecessary for a DJ to have the latest equipment if he has a good ear for music.*

B. The Right Mix

PART 1 ● Music

1 What is your favorite genre?

2 What types of songs do you listen to when you feel…

…happy? …tired?

…stressed? …excited?

> **Example:**
> What types of songs do you listen to when you feel happy?
> *Well, when I feel happy, I like to listen to music that I can dance to.*

What is a good song to represent…

…you? ….your **generation**? …your country?

3 What would be the perfect mood music for the following events?

- Studying for an exam
- Exercising
- Graduation
- Marriage
- Partying
- **Breaking Up**

- Pop
- Classical
- Rock n' Roll
- Jazz/Blues
- Hip Hop
- Dance
- New Age
- Country
- Folk

MUSIC GENRES

PART 2 ● Movie

1 What is your favorite genre?

2 What movie in particular makes you feel….

…happy?

…depressed?

…angry?

…bored?

3 Rank these things in order of importance for a movie to be good. Give a reason why you think so.

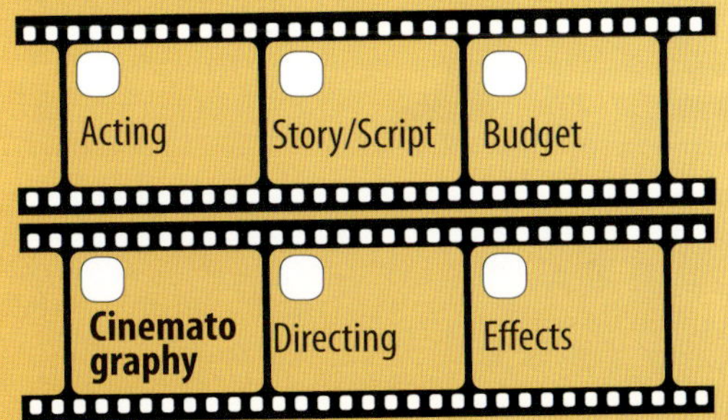

Break up (*phrasal v.*): end a relationship
Cinematography (*n.*): technique of photographing motion pictures
Generation (*n.*): people who were born at approximately the same time period

C. The Silver Screen (Now in 3D)

PART 1 ● Look at the movie posters below. What is the main genre for each? What are the subgenres?

For each poster below, make up a **synopsis** for the movie.

Include:

> How do the main characters meet or know each other?

> What is the primary conflict?

> What is the climax?

> How is the plot resolved? What is the final scene?

> Bonus: What would the sequel be?

Rated: G

Rated: R

Climax (*n.*): the most important or exciting point
Plot (*n.*): sequence of events in a novel, play, or movie
Sequel (*n.*): continuation of a story
Synopsis (*n.*): a summary of the plot

Rated: PG-13

SQUIDMAN
VS
COWBOY
ZOMBIES

Rated: R

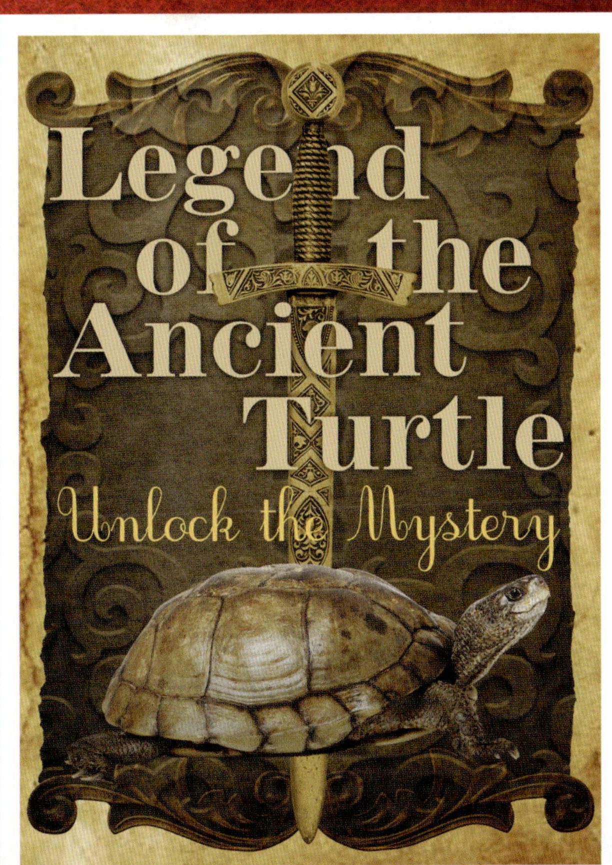

Rated: PG

Rated: PG-13

PART 2 ● Create Your Own Film

1. In a group, develop a movie of your own.
   Your movie needs:
   Title // Genre and Subgenres // **Cast** // Location // Plot // Tag Line
   If you need ideas, you can either make a sequel to one of the films on the previous page or use some of the items below to make up a new story!

Character	Plot hook	Location
Bobo the Clown	They have inherited an old mansion	The rainforest
Bam Stroker, Vampire	An almost perfect crime	A distant space colony
Valerie North, Politician	They found a bag with a million dollars	A small village in the 1800's
Jack Jax, Superstar Athlete	A science experiment has unintended consequences	An overcrowded metropolis
Samantha Shovel, Detective	An unlikely love story	A beach resort
Woofie the Wonder Dog	A family member has been kidnapped	A traveling circus

2. What will the movie poster look like?

Cast (*n.*): participants in a performance

Discussion **Questions**

1 What is your favorite movie (or one of your favorite movies) of all time?

▶ What is it that you especially like about this movie?

2 Who are some of your favorite actors and actresses?

▶ What is it that you like about them?

3 If you had the opportunity to make a movie, what kind of movie would you like to make?

4 How do you feel about the way that movies are censored?

▶ Do you think censoring should be stricter or more lenient?

5 How often do you like to **catch a flick**?

▶ What movies are playing around town right now?

▶ Which ones would you recommend?

6 Do you think you have good taste in music?

▶ Is it important for your boyfriend or girlfriend **to be into** the same kind of music?

7 Can you recommend any music that I should **check out**?

▶ What genre is it?

▶ When did you get into the singer or band?

How well can you use:

☐ Adjectives that describe art?

☐ *For* and *to* when expressing strength of opinion?

What do you need to study more?

Catch a flick (*idiom*): see a movie in a theater
Check out (*phrasal v.*): investigate
Get into (*phrasal v.*): appreciate

BONUS BONUS

Activity : And the Award Goes To...

Complete the script from a touching movie scene. Work with one or more people to fill out the chart below. One person should fill in the chart, then read it out loud.

1) Name	2) Event	3) Another name	4) Singular noun	5) Adjective
6) Adjective	7) Question	8) Occupation	9) Another occupation	10) country
11) kind of transportation	12) Number	13) Singular noun	14) Command	15) Another command
16) Object	17) Another object	18) Sound	19) Adverb	20) Superlative

Friendly Goodbyes

Scene: Sunset. Two characters are standing on the sidewalk. There is a suitcase between them.

A: I never realized that my life would be like this, 1)___________. Ever since 2)___________, everything has changed.

B: Yes, 3)___________, life is like a 4)___________. One moment, everything is 5) ___________, and the next moment, everything is 6) ___________. I've been around here for years, and I still have the same question I've always had: 7)___________?

A: That really is the question that we're all asking ourselves. Whether you're a 8)___________ or a 9)___________. I don't think that the answer is ever easy to find.

B: Anyways, now that everything is different, how long are you planning to stay in 10)___________?

A: I'll only stay here until the next 11)___________ arrives. I've got 12)___________ dollars and a 13)___________ in my suitcase. I don't think I need anything else.

B: Well, we sure are going to miss you. When you're traveling, 14)___________ and don't 15)___________. I'll give you my 16)___________ to keep you safe.

A: I can't believe that you would give that away! Here…take my 17)___________ so that you can always remember me. I won't need it when I'm starting my new life.

B: Thank you so much. I'll never forget the time we spent together. Whenever I hear 18)___________, I'll think of you 19)___________.

A: This has truly been the 20)___________ time of my life.

End Scene

Segue

ll Categories NEW SALE My Page Cart Support

'elcome to PiecePusher.com

I'm looking for... Search in all Search

ne site for buying and selling art! We've got a few new images from the local college art show. you would like to purchase an image that has already been sold, please check back for more work the same artist. more info

Artist's name: Lisa

In this painting, I wanted to represent the way I feel in my life right now. I chose lots of vivid colors because I am happy and cheerful. The green color on the right hand side of the painting is how I imagine my future to look.

$ 100

Artist's name: Jeremy Bullis

Hey art lovers! I created this piece while I was camping in the Alaskan wilderness. I wanted to capture all of the amazing natural beauty around me. I think that the piece turned out really well.

$ 50

Artist's name: N.

This image represents the way that I feel about art.

$ 1000

Artist's name: Julio Sanders

This is a sketch of N. She is the love of my life. I wanted it to be realistic. I spent hours trying to recreate the intense look in her eyes.

$ 1000

A. Discussion

1. Which of the pieces above would you be most likely to buy? Which piece would you be least likely to buy? Explain your choices.
2. Do you think that it's important to put a price on art? Why or why not?

B. Writing

Draw a picture, or select an image from a magazine or newspaper. Then, write a description of the picture and give it a price. If you don't think it's necessary to put a price on art, explain why the image is priceless.

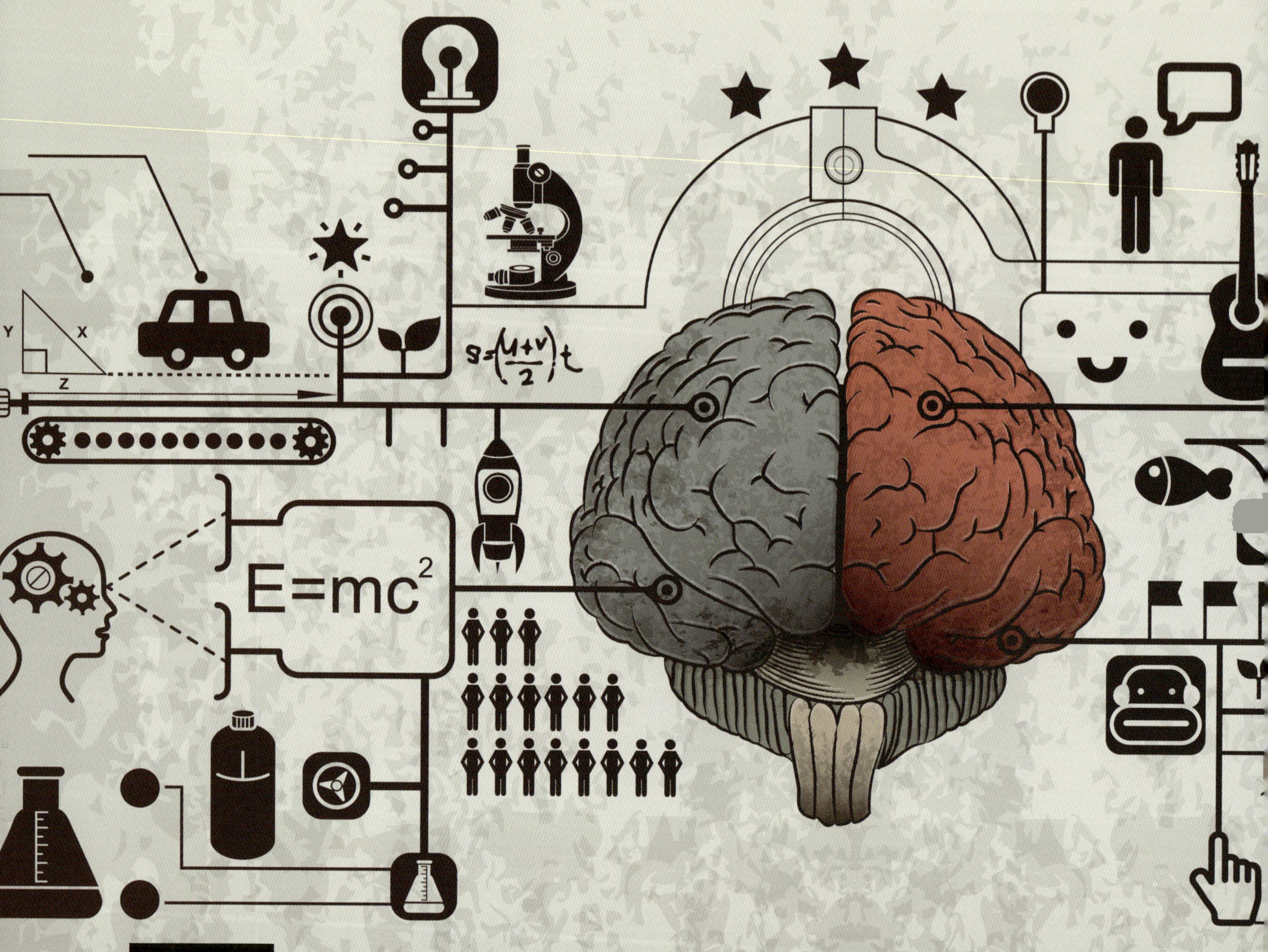

02

On the Same Page

Planning and Compromising

Objectives:

/ Talk about considerations while planning
/ Use –ever words
/ Listen to a story about an indecisive friend

WARM UP

1. What do you plan to do…

- ...this weekend?
- ...later today?
- ...on your next vacation?

2. How do you plan for…

- ...a big project?
- ...a trip overseas?
- ...a birthday party?

IDIOMS

- **Game plan**
  Before talking to your boss about the raise, you should have a *game plan*.
- **Common ground**
  We can't seem to agree on the specifics of what to do. We need to find some *common ground*.

PHRASAL VERBS

- **Plan out**
  If you have time tomorrow, we can sit down and *plan* the trip *out*.
- **Settle on**
  We have to *settle on* a place to eat soon. I'm starving!

COLLOCATIONS

- **Compromise on something with someone**
  I had to *compromise on* the specifics of the plan *with* the team so that we could move forward.
- **Come up with**
  It wasn't easy, but I *came up with* some ideas for how we can finish this project.

TONGUE TWISTER

A fly and flea flew into a flue,
Said the fly to the flea, "what shall we do?"
"Let us fly," said the flea.
Said the fly, "shall we flee?"
So they flew through a flaw in the flue.

LESSON 1

A. Decisions, Decisions

♻ • Indirect questions

PART 1

Before making a plan it is helpful to raise important considerations. Raise considerations using the following statements:

You should consider…
You need to think about…
You have to keep in mind…

Example: Camping trip in the mountains.

A: *I'm going on a camping trip in the mountains. What should I consider?*

B: *You need to think about* ***what the weather will be like****. Will it be warm or cold?*

C: *Right. You should also consider* ***where you can plug in your hairdryer****.*

A: *Oh! I hadn't thought about that! Do tents have power outlets?*

Do You Remember? - Using Indirect Questions

An indirect question is a question that functions as the object of a verb. This is useful if you want to suggest a **consideration** to someone.

What time of year is it? →

We should consider ***what time of year it is****.*

◇ Note: In an indirect question, the subject comes before the verb.

What are some important considerations to make in the situations below?

Camping trip in the mountains

1. What time of year is it?
   You should consider what time of year it is.
2.
3.

Applying to a university

1. What do you want to study?
   You need to think about what you want to study.
2.
3.

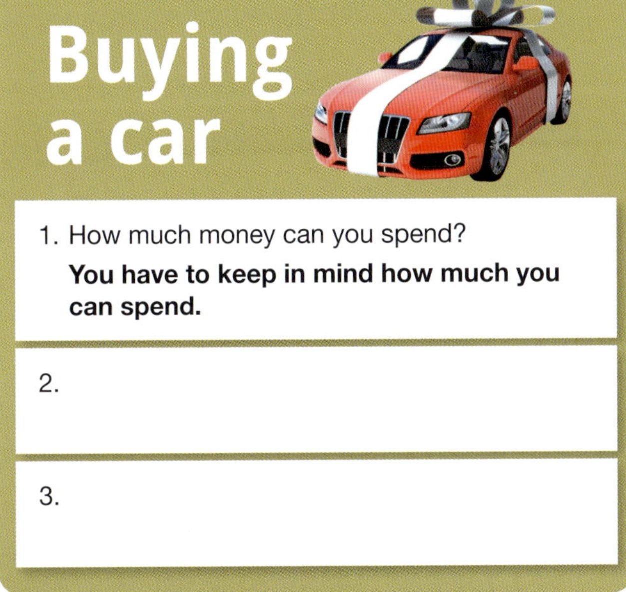

Buying a car

1. How much money can you spend?
   You have to keep in mind how much you can spend.
2.
3.

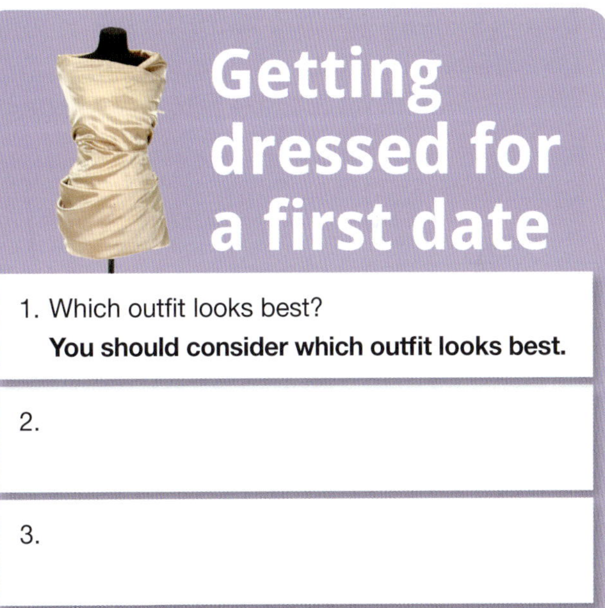

Getting dressed for a first date

1. Which outfit looks best?
   You should consider which outfit looks best.
2.
3.

Write down something you would like to do:

1.
2.
3.

consideration (*n.*): careful thought

B. Whatever's Clever

Language Point : "-ever" Words

Words ending with –ever can be used to refer to something that is undecided or unknown.

Example:

Whoever *wants to come is welcome.*

Wherever *you're going, have fun!*

We can go to eat ***whatever*** *you want.*

Would you rather go by taxi or subway? We can go ***however*** *you want.*

Tip The expression "whatever", when used as a response, expresses disinterest and can often sound rude.

A: *I don't approve of what you're wearing, young lady.*

B: *Whatever.*

Pre-listening

1. Do you think it's safe to travel wherever you want? Why or why not?
2. Can you get along with whoever you meet? Why or why not?
3. What is something you take with you whenever you go out?

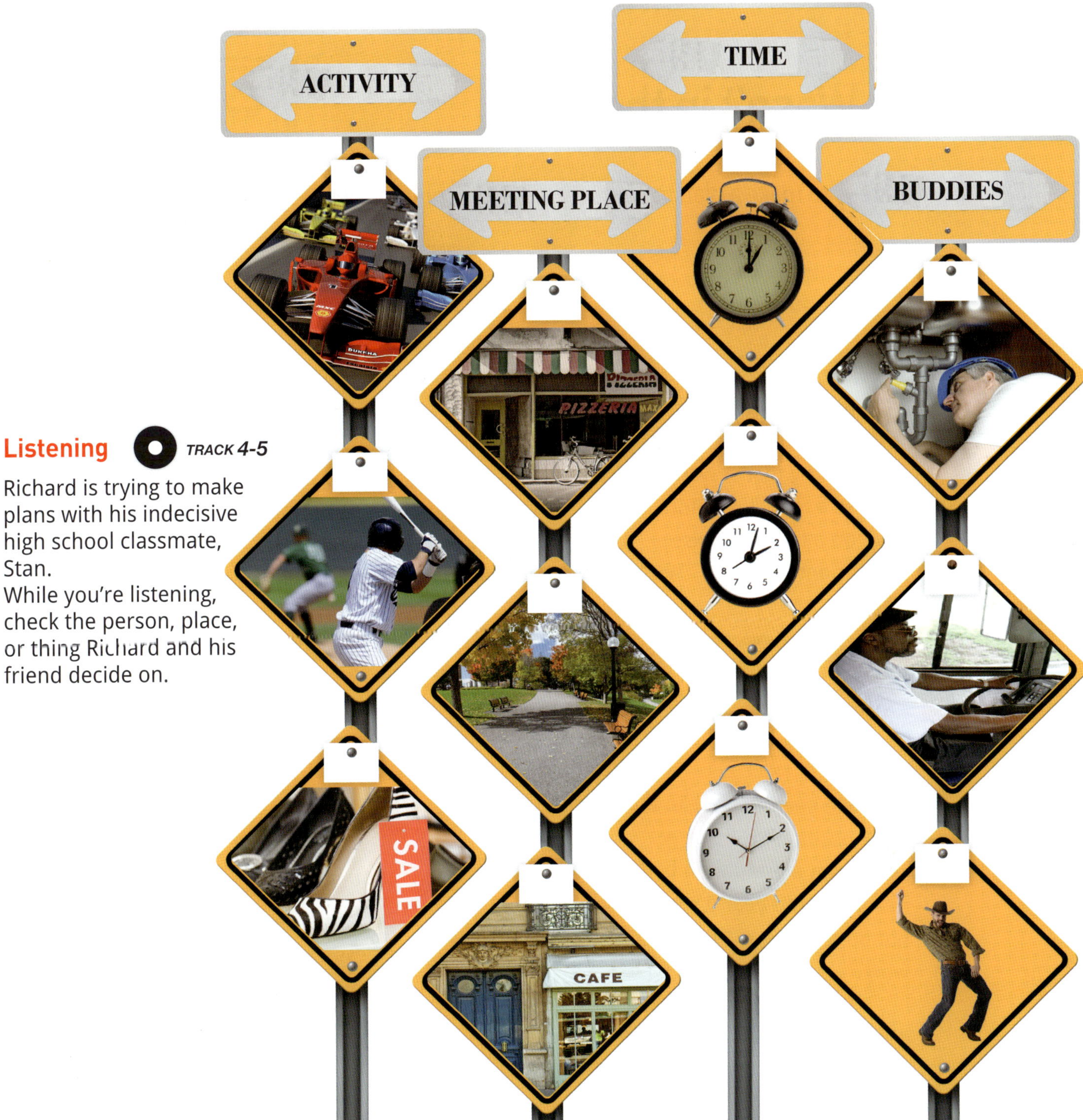

Listening

TRACK 4-5

Richard is trying to make plans with his indecisive high school classmate, Stan.
While you're listening, check the person, place, or thing Richard and his friend decide on.

Post-listening

When reacting to –ever words it's good to follow up with a suggestion.

How about……?
What about……?
What if…….?
Why don't…….?

Take turns starting conversations and responding with indecisive –ever answers. Ask a follow-up question to try to narrow down the plan.

- Where would you like to go for dinner?
- What do you want to do after class?
- Who should we call to come to the party?
- When would you like to go on vacation?
- How do you want to get there?

C. This Wasn't in the Plan.

Follow the steps to make a plan to solve each of the problems below.

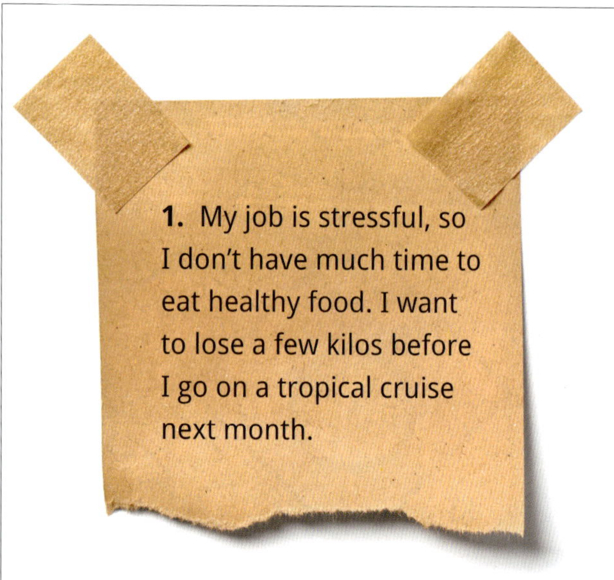

Steps to Solving a Problem:

a) First, identify a problem.
The problem is...

b) Then, brainstorm possible solutions.
For one possible solution, this person could...

c) After that, weigh the pros and cons of each solution.
Taking a cooking class would be good because...

d) Finally, choose a solution and develop a realistic timetable to solve the problem!
Okay, so first he should register for a cooking class. Then, he should try to attend the class as much as possible...

2. I have been working in the same position for three years, and I want a promotion before the end of this year. I work hard, but no one seems to notice my work.

3. There's a girl that I really like, but she doesn't even know who I am.

4. I have one year left of high school, and I want to get into a good university. My parents want me to study art, but I'd really like to major in history.

5. Now, think of a problem that you've been having in your own life. Use the problem solving steps to figure out a solution.

Discussion Questions

1 What are some important things to consider before planning a trip?

2 Do you like planning out a trip before you go, or do you prefer that someone else take care of all the details? Why?

3 How important is it to have a game plan when traveling to…

- …somewhere in your city?
- …somewhere in your country?
- …to a foreign country?

4 How hard is it for you to come up with a plan when you're bored?

- What do you usually do when you have a hard time deciding on a plan?
- Do you know anyone who always says "whatever you want" to a suggestion?

5 What plans do you have for yourself in the short term?

- What plans do you have for yourself in the long term?

6 Do you use a calendar or planner?

- What are the best ways to remember what you have to do?

7 Do you try to make plans every weekend? Why or why not?

8 What things in life are impossible to plan for?

come up with (*phrasal v.*): to produce or discover something
common ground (*n.*): something mutually agreed upon
game plan (*n.*): a strategy to achieve a goal
settle on (*phrasal v.*): to solve a problem

LESSON 2

>> WARM UP

Objectives:

/ Negotiate and compromise while planning

Uh-oh! Looks like you've got too much stuff to do in one day. Assuming you can only pick **three** of the things to do today and that you must put off the rest, which three would you choose? Why?

- Call telecom company about problem on phone bill.
- Visit Grandma's house and move some furniture around.
- Have lunch with best friend who lives out of town.
- Go to gym for a couple of hours.
- Buy professor/boss a birthday gift.
- Blind date with someone your friend says is "really cute"
- Watch season finale of favorite TV show.
- Last day to return a jacket you bought, but don't really like.
- Go to dentist for check up.

A. I Didn't Think This Through

Look at the situations below. Identify which step or steps were missed in planning. What should they have done differently and how could they have changed the situation?

Do You Remember? Expressing Regret and Advice in the Past

Should + **Have** + **Past Participle** expresses regret or hindsight advice.

It's really snowing. I should have planned for bad weather.

Could + **Have** + **Past Participle** expresses choices that were not made.

I could have looked at the forecast on the Internet.

Lionel's new garage is on the second floor.

It poured at Chip and Janet's wedding.

Abbie and Abby wore the same dress.

Carl could not pay for lunch.

Ernest is out of gas on the highway.

Andrea forgot to bring a pencil to an exam.

There wasn't enough food at Joy's party.

Jimbo forgot to make reservations.

pour (*v.*): to rain very heavily

B. Negotiation Station

Language Point : Negotiating and Compromising

Negotiating

- If I **A**, then will you **B**?
  If I buy the food, then will you get the drinks?
- **Would you be willing to...**
  Would you be willing to go to a Mexican restaurant instead?
- But if I **A**, then you should **B**,
  Okay, but if I go to a Mexican restaurant, then you should pay.

Compromising

That's fair. / That's fine. / That'll be okay.

That's not fair. / That's no good. I'd rather...

PART 1 ● With a partner match the numbers to the letters to express a negotiation. Then say if you think the deal is fair or not. If you don't think the situation is fair, negotiate a compromise.

Example: If you make the presentation,

A: *If you make the presentation, I'll give it to the boss.*

B: *That's not fair. I have to do way more work.*

A: *Would you be willing to give the presentation instead?*

B: *That's no good. I hate speaking in front of people. Will you help me edit the presentation if I write it?*

A: *That's fine.*

1. If you promise to pay me back with interest,
2. If you aren't here by the time the show starts,
3. I'll buy popcorn and drinks
4. If you don't stop drinking so much,
5. I'll go to Europe with you
6. If you clean the bathroom,

A. I'll leave the ticket with the box office.
B. I'm not going out with you anymore.
C. I'll loan you the money.
D. I'll do the laundry.
E. if you drive to the theater.
F. if you agree to stay in hotels.

negotiate ***(v.)*:** to attempt to come to an agreement on something

PART 2

You and your partner have made plans to do the following things, and must work out the details. Take turns starting the discussion. If you disagree, you should negotiate a compromise.

STUDENT A

Plan to see a movie

1: You want to see a ______ (genre)______ movie.

> **Example**: *I'd like to see a western. What do you think?*

3: You want to see the movie at ______(location)______ at______(time)______.

5: You need to agree on who is going to pay for the tickets and who is going to get the snacks

6: You would also like.....

Final plan:

Type of movie: ______________.

Time: ______________.

Food: ______________.

Set roommate boundaries

2: You would prefer to live in __(city/area)__ because______.

4: If the apartment is $1000 a month, your share should be ___________.

6: You think each person should be responsible for __(chores)__

8: You think that....

Final plan:

Location: ______________.

Paying rent: ______________.

Chores: ______________.

Go on an island getaway

1: You would like to visit __ (island) __ for ___(length of time)___

3: You think that __(amount of money)____ is enough per person.

5: You want to see _____ (famous site)__

7: You would also like...

Final plan:

Location/Season: ______________.

Budget: ______________.

Activities: ______________.

Sightseeing: ______________.

Food: ______________.

You and your partner have made plans to do the following things, and must work out the details. Take turns starting the discussion. If you disagree, you should negotiate a compromise.

STUDENT B

Plan to see a movie

2: You would rather see a ______(genre)______ movie.

> **Example**: *Actually, I'd rather see a romantic comedy. (negotiate a compromise)*

4: You want to see the movie at ______(location)______ at______(time)______.

6: You want to eat ______ (snacks)______ at the movie.

8: You think that...

Final plan:

Type of movie: ______________.

Time: ______________.

Food: ______________.

Set roommate boundaries

1: You want to live in ______(city/area)______ because______.

3: You want the ______(big/ small)______ room.

5: You want to ______(share/ not share)______ food.

7: You would also like...

Final plan:

Location: ______________.

Paying rent: ______________.

Chores: ______________.

Go on an island getaway

2: You would rather go to ______(island) ______ in ______(time of year)______

4: You would like to ______ (activities) ______

6: You want to eat ______ (dish)______

8: You think that.......

Final plan:

Location/Season: ______________.

Budget: ______________.

Activities: ______________.

Sightseeing: ______________.

Food: ______________.

C. Project Plan

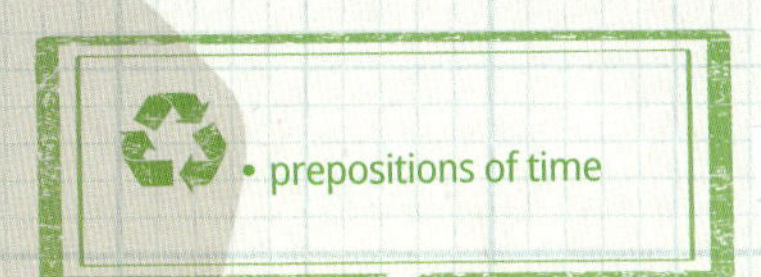

You are working on a big project together!

- You need to schedule **eight hours** of time when you can meet to research, write a paper, and create a presentation for class.
- The project is due on Friday at 10 PM.
- You must work on the project together… which means that you will need to make some compromises in your busy schedules!

3rd wheel

Listen to what Student A and Student B are saying and suggest possible compromises that you think could be made.

Example:

A: *I have some free time on Monday from 12 to 3. Can you work on the project then?*

B: *No…I have to work at my part-time job from 12 to 1 and then I have a chemistry lab. On Wednesday, I volunteer as a tutor from 1 to 5, but I can cancel that.*

A: *Oh…I definitely can't do that. I have to meet a friend for coffee from 1 to 3.*

B: *That's not fair. If I can cancel tutoring, can you cancel your coffee date?*

STUDENT A

	Monday	Tuesday	Wednesday	Thursday	Friday
8:00 AM	Morning Yoga Class 8 - 9 AM		Morning Yoga Class 8 - 9 AM		Morning Yoga Class 8 - 9 AM
9:00 AM		Morning Yoga Class 9 - 10AM		Morning Yoga Class 9 - 10 AM	
10:00 AM 11:00 AM	Math 2 10 AM - 12 PM	Math 2 10 AM - 12 PM	Math 2 (quiz today) 10 AM - 12 PM	Math 2 10 AM - 12 PM	Math 2 10 AM - 12 PM
12:00 PM		Lunch date 12 - 2 PM		Anthropology study group (exam on Friday) 12 - 2 PM	Anthropology study group (exam today) 12 - 2 PM
1:00 PM			Meet a friend who is only in town for one day 1 - 3 PM		
2:00 PM				Work at the library (reading stories to children) 2 - 5 PM	
3:00 PM	Anthropology 3 3 - 5 PM		Anthropology 3 3 - 5 PM		Anthropology 3 (exam today) 3 - 5 PM
4:00 PM					
5:00 PM	Work at Part-Time Job 5 -10 PM	Biology Lab (test today) 5 - 8 PM	Work at Part-Time Job 5 -10 PM	Biology Lab 5 - 8 PM	Work at Part-Time Job 5 -10 PM
6:00 PM					
7:00 PM					
8:00 PM		Feed a friend's dogs 8 - 10 PM		Go to a birthday dinner for your best friend 8 -10 PM	
9:00 PM					

anthropology ***(n.)***: the study of humankind

You are working on a big project together!

- You need to schedule **eight hours** of time when you can meet to research, write a paper, and create a presentation for class.
- The project is due on Friday at 10 PM.
- You must work on the project together… which means that you will need to make some compromises in your busy schedules!

3rd wheel

Listen to what Student A and Student B are saying and suggest possible compromises that you think could be made.

Example:

A: *I have some free time on Monday from 12 to 3. Can you work on the project then?*

B: *No…I have to work at my part-time job from 12 to 1 and then I have a chemistry lab. On Wednesday, I volunteer as a tutor from 1 to 5, but I can cancel that.*

A: *Oh…I definitely can't do that. I have to meet a friend for coffee from 1 to 3.*

B: *That's not fair. If I can cancel tutoring, can you cancel your coffee date?*

STUDENT B

	Monday	Tuesday	Wednesday	Thursday	Friday
8:00 AM					
9:00 AM	Psychology 1 9-10 AM	Psychology 1 9-10 AM	Psychology 1 9-10 AM	Psychology 1 9-10 AM	Psychology 1 9-10 AM
10:00 AM	Work at Part-Time Job 10 AM – 1 PM	Work at Part-Time Job 10 AM – 1 PM	Work at Part-Time Job 10 AM – 1 PM	Work at Part-Time Job 10 AM – 1 PM	Work at Part-Time Job 10 AM – 1 PM
11:00 AM					
12:00 PM					
1:00 PM	Chemistry Lab 1 - 5 PM	Chemistry Lab (test today) 1 - 5 PM	Volunteer work: tutoring at a local school 1 - 5 PM	Volunteer work: tutoring at a local school 1 - 5 PM	Championship soccer tournament with friends 1 - 5 PM
2:00 PM					
3:00 PM					
4:00 PM					
5:00 PM	English Composition 3 5 - 7 PM		English Composition 3 5 - 7 PM	French study session 5 - 7PM	English Composition 3 5 - 7 PM
6:00 PM					
7:00 PM	Blind date with someone you've been wanting to meet 7 - 10 PM	French 4 7 - 9 PM	French 4 7 - 9 PM	French 4 7 - 9 PM	
8:00 PM					
9:00 PM					

Discussion **Questions**

1 Have you ever been in a situation where you had overlapping plans and found it very difficult to cancel either one?

2 When confronted with several options, do you find it very difficult to **settle on** one choice?

3 Do you think you are generally good at sticking to plans? What makes you say so?

4 Some people are **flaky** and don't follow through on plans. Do you know anyone like this?

- ▶ How does this kind of behavior make you feel?
- ▶ What kinds of reasons do you think are acceptable, and which ones do you think are not?

5 What is the most important plan you have made?

- ▶ Did you achieve the result you desired?
- ▶ What could you have done differently?

6 Do you think it's difficult to find **common ground** when you are working with others?

- ▶ Would you consider yourself to be a leader or a follower?
- ▶ How important is it to negotiate on a plan?

7 How do you deal with someone that refuses to compromise?

UNIT 2
REVIEW

How well can you use:

☐ Indirect question format to discuss considerations?

☐ -ever words?

☐ Expressions to talk about compromise?

What do you need to study more?

flaky ***(adj.)*:** an unreliable person
settle on ***(phrasal verb)*:** to solve a problem
common ground ***(n.)*:** something mutually agreed upon

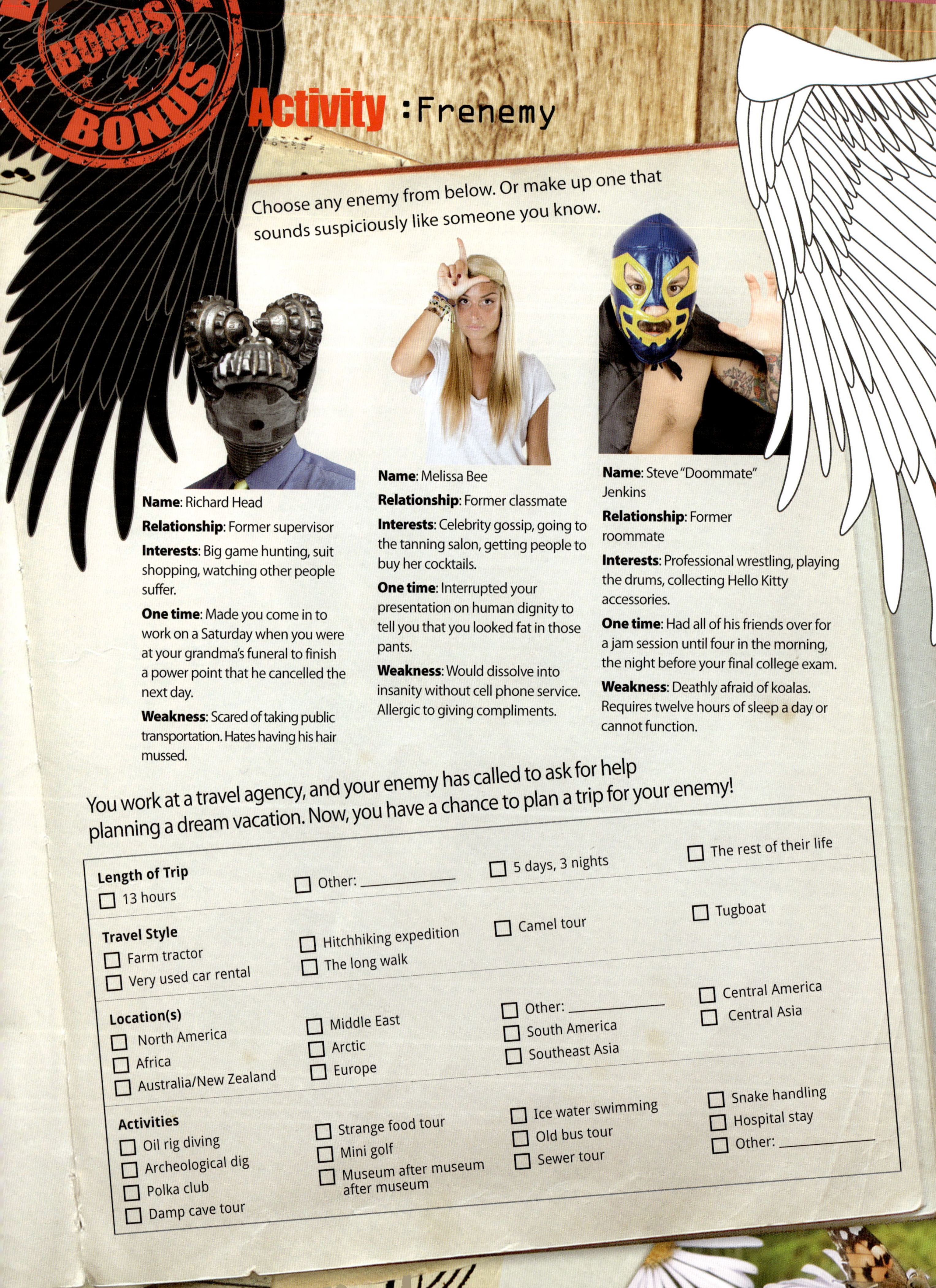

Activity : Frenemy

Choose any enemy from below. Or make up one that sounds suspiciously like someone you know.

Name: Richard Head

Relationship: Former supervisor

Interests: Big game hunting, suit shopping, watching other people suffer.

One time: Made you come in to work on a Saturday when you were at your grandma's funeral to finish a power point that he cancelled the next day.

Weakness: Scared of taking public transportation. Hates having his hair mussed.

Name: Melissa Bee

Relationship: Former classmate

Interests: Celebrity gossip, going to the tanning salon, getting people to buy her cocktails.

One time: Interrupted your presentation on human dignity to tell you that you looked fat in those pants.

Weakness: Would dissolve into insanity without cell phone service. Allergic to giving compliments.

Name: Steve "Doommate" Jenkins

Relationship: Former roommate

Interests: Professional wrestling, playing the drums, collecting Hello Kitty accessories.

One time: Had all of his friends over for a jam session until four in the morning, the night before your final college exam.

Weakness: Deathly afraid of koalas. Requires twelve hours of sleep a day or cannot function.

You work at a travel agency, and your enemy has called to ask for help planning a dream vacation. Now, you have a chance to plan a trip for your enemy!

Length of Trip
- ☐ 13 hours
- ☐ Other: ________
- ☐ 5 days, 3 nights
- ☐ The rest of their life

Travel Style
- ☐ Farm tractor
- ☐ Very used car rental
- ☐ Hitchhiking expedition
- ☐ The long walk
- ☐ Camel tour
- ☐ Tugboat

Location(s)
- ☐ North America
- ☐ Africa
- ☐ Australia/New Zealand
- ☐ Middle East
- ☐ Arctic
- ☐ Europe
- ☐ Other: ________
- ☐ South America
- ☐ Southeast Asia
- ☐ Central America
- ☐ Central Asia

Activities
- ☐ Oil rig diving
- ☐ Archeological dig
- ☐ Polka club
- ☐ Damp cave tour
- ☐ Strange food tour
- ☐ Mini golf
- ☐ Museum after museum after museum
- ☐ Ice water swimming
- ☐ Old bus tour
- ☐ Sewer tour
- ☐ Snake handling
- ☐ Hospital stay
- ☐ Other: ________

http://www.Stan's-Blog.com

Stan's Blog: A Blog about Stuff

Hey guys. It's me, Stan. I guess you know that because it's my blog. So I thought about writing something today. I don't really know what to write about. So. I guess I can just write about…stuff.

Alright, so the first bit of stuff today is my buddy Richard. Man, that guy needs to calm down. Richard, if you're reading this, I'm only saying it as a friend. Calm down. You don't always need to have a plan to have a good time. Sometimes, I just want to go out and get lost. Maybe something exciting will happen along the way! Just because I don't say, "Hey, I know what stuff I want to do!" doesn't mean I don't have opinions. I have opinions, too. I just don't say them like other people.

That leads me to my second bit of stuff. I want people to be happy. I like people and I like it when they're happy. That makes sense, right? So if people—let's say Richard, for example—give some options for things they like to do…well, then I am happy to do whatever makes them happy. That's polite, right? I was visiting Richard in his town. I don't know what's fun in his town. Why should I have to decide what to do? I might make a terrible decision and then none of us would enjoy ourselves. Heck, it might be such a terrible decision that it ruins my visit. It could even ruin our friendship. It could be the worst decision I've ever made, AND MY ENTIRE LIFE COULD BE RUINED!

I CAN'T MAKE THOSE KINDS OF DECISIONS, RICHARD!

Oh…LOL. Sorry about that, folks. I must have hit the caps lock key. I think it's my favorite key on the keyboard.

So. I guess that's about all I have for today's blog. I was thinking about some other stuff, but I guess it can wait. As always, I'd be happy to hear from anyone out there who is reading my blog. But don't feel like you have to…it's just a suggestion. :)

A. Discussion

1. How does Stan feel about his relationship with Richard? What could Stan and Richard do to improve their relationship?
2. Do you agree with Stan's thoughts about making plans? Why or why not? Would you consider yourself to be a person who likes to make plans ahead of time, or do you prefer spontaneity?

B. Writing

Take a stand! Write a blog post about either the importance of making firm decisions OR the benefit of letting other people choose what they want to do first.

03 Above and Beyond

Responsibilities

Objectives:

- Talk about fulfilling life's responsibilities
- Listen to a conversation about productivity at work

WARM UP

What responsibilities do you have in the following areas?

- Your country
- Education
- Your family
- Place of work
- Your social life

IDIOMS

- **Hold someone accountable**

  If we lose this game, I know my team is going to *hold me accountable.*
- **Bite off more than you can chew**

  Don't *bite off more than you can chew*. Ask someone for help if you need it.

PHRASAL VERBS

- **Own up**

  You should just *own up* to your mistake.
- **Back out**

  You agreed to work for me this Saturday. Please don't *back out now.*

COLLOCATIONS

- **Heavy responsibility**

  When I was young, I had to watch my brother and sister. It was a really *heavy responsibility.*

- **Deny it**

  Don't try to *deny it*. I know you're the one who didn't turn off the lights.

LESSON 1

A. Responsible Slacker Quiz

Answer the questions to the quiz below to find out who's more responsible! Explain your choices.

01

How do you feel about responsibility?

- ☐ It gives me a purpose. (3 POINTS)
- ☐ It's just a part of life. (2 POINTS)
- ☐ I avoid it whenever I can. (1 POINT)

02

Lead or follow?

- ☐ Lead. (3 POINTS)
- ☐ Lead only if I have to. (2 POINTS)
- ☐ Follow. (1 POINT)

03

How often do you exercise?

- ☐ Several times a week. (3 POINTS)
- ☐ A few times a month. (2 POINTS)
- ☐ I sometimes have to walk from the couch to the refrigerator. (1 POINT)

04

You have a project due in a month.

- ☐ Immediately outline a plan and begin work. (3 POINTS)
- ☐ Put it on my "to do" list and start working on it when I have time. (2 POINTS)
- ☐ A month is a long time – I'll do it a day or two before the deadline. (1 POINT)

05

Have you ever cheated on something?

- ☐ Of course not! (3 POINTS)
- ☐ Maybe once or twice, but nothing major. (2 POINTS)
- ☐ Whenever I can. If I get the chance, why not take it? (1 POINT)

06

You wake up feeling a little sick.

- ☐ Go to work/class anyway! I only stay home if I'm about to die. (3 POINTS)
- ☐ Try to go out, but if I continue to feel sick, go back home. (2 POINTS)
- ☐ Not going to risk it. Call in and try to sound extra sick when I talk to my boss. (1 POINT)

07

What's your diet like?

- [ ] I make sure to always eat healthy meals and avoid fast food. (3 POINTS)
- [ ] I do my best to eat healthy now and again, but I also enjoy fatty foods. (2 POINTS)
- [ ] I eat whatever's quickest, so lots of fast food and street vendors. (1 POINT)

08

Do you always keep your promises and commitments?

- [ ] Of course. A person is only as good as their word. (3 POINTS)
- [ ] Most of the time I try, but it's not always possible. (2 POINTS)
- [ ] Don't blame me - I'm a very busy person! If it's really important, I will get around to it. (1 POINT)

09

Do you have goals?

- [ ] I set clear goals so that I can always keep them. (3 POINTS)
- [ ] I have goals, but I have a hard time sticking to them. (2 POINTS)
- [ ] Life is too unpredictable to limit myself to specific goals. (1 POINT)

10

Do you admit your mistakes?

- [ ] Admitting mistakes is the best way to learn from them. (3 POINTS)
- [ ] Only if someone catches me. I don't want to look bad! (2 POINTS)
- [ ] I don't make mistakes, and if I did, I definitely wouldn't tell anybody! (1 POINT)

11

Do you use speech to encourage others?

- [ ] I compliment people frequently and tell them when they've done a good job. (3 POINTS)
- [ ] If I think someone really needs a **pick-me-up**. Or if it helps me earn points at work. (2 POINTS)
- [ ] I don't think I'm that good at telling people positive things. (1 POINT)

12

You've been trying to save money but you just found an amazing deal on a new phone.

- [ ] A phone would be nice, but having money saved is even nicer. (3 POINTS)
- [ ] Well, maybe I'd be paying a little bit now, but I'd be saving money on the phone, right? (2 POINTS)
- [ ] Buy the phone! I was never good at saving anyway... (1 POINT)

Score

34 – 36: SAINTHOOD You're super responsible. Just don't have a heart attack along the way.

29 – 33: ON TOP OF IT People look to you as a responsible person worthy of respect.

21 – 28: WELL-BALANCED Not too stressed, not too irresponsible, how do you manage it?

15 – 20: MASTER SLACKER You lead a carefree life and you're not tied down to anything!

12 – 14: DO YOU HAVE A PULSE? Maybe you should...nah, you wouldn't do it anyway.

Do you agree with the results of the quiz?
Would you consider yourself a responsible person?

pick-me-up (*idiom.*): a small something that gives you energy
call in (*phrasal v.*): to call and tell work you are not coming
pulse (*n.*): regular beat of blood flow
slacker (*n.*): somebody who avoids working

B. I'll Stop Procrastinating... Tomorrow.

Pre-listening

1. If someone were to observe you working or studying, which of the following things would they see?

2. Which of the above habits are productive and which are irresponsible? Why do you think so?

Listening TRACK 6-7

Richard is having a meeting with an "Efficiency Expert" at work. While listening, circle the letter (from above) of the point they are discussing.

Post-listening

1. Which of the things above does Richard think make him a responsible employee? Do you agree?

2. What two things do you do that make you a productive or responsible person? What things do you do that are irresponsible or lazy? Be honest.

procrastinate (*v.*): to postpone doing something

C. See It My Way

PART 1 ● **A consultant** has come to your office to help improve efficiency and set responsibilities. Take turns playing the roles of consultant and employee on the next two pages.

- If you are the consultant, ask the employee about the notes you have on them.
- If you are the employee, try to clarify your weak points, and contrast them with your strong points.
  After role-playing, the consultant must decide whether the employee deserves a promotion.

Example:

Employee: *Hi, I'm Richard! I work in the Marketing department.*

Consultant: *Hi Richard. So, when I was observing, I noticed that you seem to spread yourself between many tasks. Why is that?*

Employee: *Well, I think I'm good at multi-tasking.*

Consultant: *Really? Why do you think it takes you so long to finish projects?*

3rd wheel

Act as an irresponsible consultant. Whatever advice the consultant gives, follow up with some bad advice.

Consultant's Notes.
Name: Richard
Department: Marketing

- Spread between too many tasks
- Takes a really long time to finish projects

Employee: Richard.
Department: Marketing

- Stays late to finish projects
- Perfectionist
- Great team player

STUDENT A

① **Consultant's Notes**
Name: Alex
Department: Advertising

- Rarely attends staff meetings and staff birthday parties
- Spends a lot of time talking on the phone and messaging

Promotion? yes / no

② **Employee: Susan**
Department: Design

- Quickly comes up with design ideas
- Sometimes has trouble paying attention to details

③ **Consultant's Notes**
Name: Derek

- Often late for work
- Rarely in his office

Promotion? yes / no

STUDENT B

Employee: Alex
Department: Advertising

- Consistently meets deadlines
- Spends much of the day contacting designers about advertising designs

Consultant's Notes
Name: Susan
Department: Design

- Frequently misses project deadline
- Starts many projects, but leaves others to finish them

Promotion? yes / no

Employee: Derek
Department: Human Resources

- Drops his kids off at school every morning but works late most evenings
- Walks around to talk with colleagues face to face

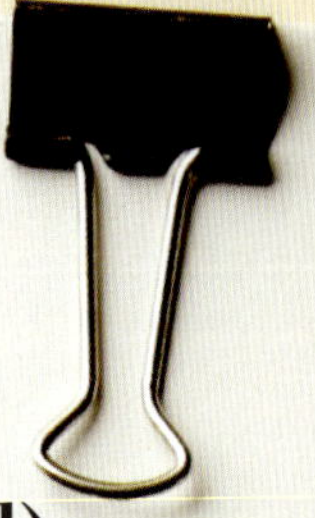

STUDENT A (continued)

④

Consultant's Notes
Name: Lynn
Branch Manager

- Spends much of the day sitting in her office chatting with employees
- Exceeds her budget for social events every month

Promotion? yes / no

⑤

Consultant's Notes
Name: John
Department: Design

- Is a slow worker
- Does not take feedback on his work well

Promotion? yes / no

⑥

Employee: Jenny
Department: Accounting

- Always early for work
- Popular among coworkers; people often ask her for advice because she is very knowledgeable about accounting

STUDENT B (continued)

Employee: Lynn
Branch Manager

- Employees believe that she is a fun, friendly manager
- Frequently has parties in the office to recognize workers' achievements

Employee: John
Department: Design

- Spends a lot of time carefully designing products
- Shy and sensitive about his work, but tries to make revisions when asked

Consultant's Notes
Name: Jenny
Department: Accounting

- Takes very long lunch breaks
- Spends much of the day chatting with coworkers

Promotion? yes / no

PART 2 ● With your partner, review the employees you selected for possible promotions. Choose one employee for a final promotion.

Compare your choice with your classmates' choices. Choose one employee as a class for the promotion.

Discussion Questions

1 Is there anything that you are supposed to get done by the end of today?

▶ How about by the end of the week?

▶ Do you think you will get these things done?

2 What are the most important responsibilities for…

▶ …children?

▶ …parents?

▶ …university students?

▶ …part-time workers?

3 What are the responsibilities of a father to his family?

▶ What are the responsibilities of a mother to her family?

4 What do you think of people who are always **backing out** of their responsibilities by not doing their fair share of work or not paying their bills?

5 Who is the most irresponsible person you know?

▶ Who is the most responsible person you know?

6 Do you ever feel that you have too many responsibilities?

▶ Have you ever tried to **bite off more than you could chew**? What happened?

7 How old should someone be before they are considered responsible for their own actions?

▶ Do you think you are completely responsible for yourself, or does someone take care of you in some way?

8 Are you good at **owning up** to your mistakes? Why do you think so?

▶ Why do you think people try to deny it even when it is clear they are to blame?

---

bite off more than you can chew *(idiom.)*: to try to do more than you are able to do
own up *(phrasal v.)*: to admit to having done something

LESSON 2

>> WARM UP

Objectives:

/ Describe responsibilities and expectations

What responsibilities do these people have to you?

Strangers
Relatives
Significant Other
Neighbors
Teacher

A. Let's Talk Responsibility

Language Point : Talking about Expectations

Be supposed to is used to talk about responsibilities...	**Be expected to** is used to talk about correct procedures...
▸ *I am supposed to finish this report by five p.m.*	▸ *You're not expected to bring anything special to the party.*
...and scheduled events.	...and duties.
▸ *The game is supposed to start any minute.*	▸ *All citizens are expected to do military service.*

PART 1 ● Look at the situations below and ask questions about responsibilities connected to them. Answer with your opinion on what you are expected to or not supposed to do in that situation.

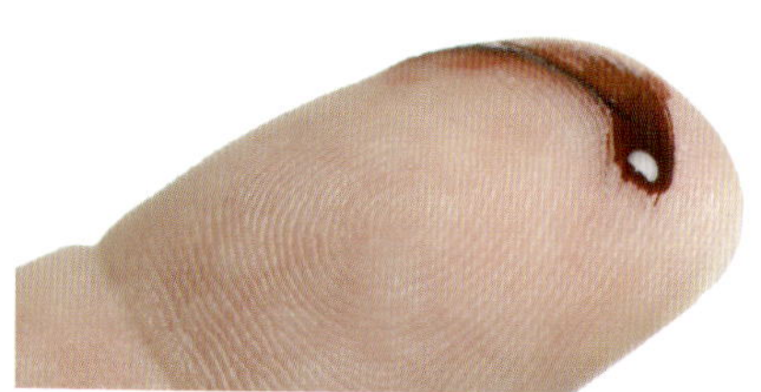
Cut yourself

Example:

A: *What are you supposed to do if you **cut yourself**?*

B: *Well, you are supposed to wash the wound with soap and water.*

C: *You're supposed to go to the hospital if the cut is deep and doesn't stop bleeding.*

1 Losing or finding a wallet

2 In class

3 Leaving the house

4 On the subway

5 Getting in shape

6 Visiting someone's home

***Be supposed to** is used in the past tense to express something that was expected but did not happen, or an unfulfilled responsibility.*

You were supposed to be here twenty minutes ago! Now we'll probably miss the beginning of the movie.
The game is supposed to start any minute.

PART 2 ● Brainstorm the things these people were supposed to do and forgot, or were not supposed to do and regret.

Example: Officer Dan is chasing down the Chicken Man.

A: *It seems like Officer Dan was supposed to be watching the armored car. Instead, he was out buying a donut.*

B: *It looks like the Chicken Man wasn't supposed to take the money and run.*

1

Grandpa feels sick.

1. What do you think Grandpa was supposed to do and forgot?
2. What do you think Dr. Doogie was not supposed to do and regrets?

2

Sam and Diane have to give a presentation.

1. What was Sam not supposed to do last night and regrets?
2. What was Diane supposed to do and forgot?

3

Peggy is trying to cook a nice dinner.

1. What was Peggy supposed to do but forgot?
2. What wasn't Peggy supposed to do and regrets?

4

It's Ralph and Alice's Anniversary.

1. What was Ralph supposed to do but probably forgot?
2. Or, what was Alice supposed to do for Ralph and didn't?

B. Do the Right Thing

Choose a reaction to each of the following situations from the Reaction Bank. Many reactions may be correct in each situation, but each response can only be used once. After choosing a reaction, discuss:

- Is my reaction a responsible or irresponsible one? Why?
- What are people typically supposed to or expected to do in each situation?
- What might be the consequences of my reaction?

> **Example:** I see someone being pickpocketed on the subway.
>
> **A:** *I would yell at the thief.*
>
> **B:** *Don't you think it's dangerous to confront a pickpocket? You're only supposed to call the police.*

1 Someone I have never met just made a loud, rude comment about my clothing while I was walking down the street.

2 My spouse and I got into a fight yesterday because I arrived home late. Now, he/she won't answer my messages.

3 My roommate is very noisy.

4 One of my coworkers keeps making inappropriate jokes in the office. No one has spoken up, but I can tell that people are offended.

5 This is the third month that my company has not paid me on time.

6 I accidently parked in someone else's assigned parking space. He started yelling at me.

7 I am walking with a friend when she suddenly tosses her empty coffee cup on the sidewalk and says, "Someone will pick that up later."

8 My sibling just borrowed my MP3 player for the day and left it on my desk...but now it's broken!

9 My friend has begun to complain constantly about how "ugly" he is. I think that his appearance is perfectly fine.

10 I am having a terrible day, and I just snapped at my friend while we were waiting for a third friend to arrive.

Reaction Bank

a. Apologize

b. Act confused and walk away

c. Yell at them

d. Ignore them

e. Confront them

f. Run away

g. Pretend that nothing is wrong

h. Call the police

i. Give them a lecture about the terrible thing that they did

j. Smile and compliment

k. Talk to them privately

C. We Built This City

PART 1 ● The Wasteland

1. You and your class are the City Council for the City of Cityville. What problems do you see? Which Department do you think is primarily responsible for finding a solution to that problem?
2. Rank these five areas in order of most important to the prosperity of a city. 5 = most important, 1 = least important.

PART 2 ● The People Have Voted

Using the ranks given in Part 1, you will now choose which **bills** to implement in order to improve your city.

- The rank you gave equals the amount of points you have to spend for each department. (**Example:** If you gave Education the Rank of 5, you have 5 points to spend now on Education.)
- Bills in the left column cost 1 point. Bills in the right column cost 2 points.
- Discuss the benefit that you think each bill would have on the city's problems.

1 Point	2 Point
Department of Transportation	
Bill to add a toll road	Bill to extend subway and public transportation routes
Bill to require annual Driver's Ed courses	Bill to hire additional traffic officers
Department of Education	
Bill to offer extra after school tutoring	Bill to hire new teachers
Bill to pay teachers overtime for fine arts after school activities	Bill to build new educational performance hall for each school district
Department of Security	
Bill to start program to raise drug and gang awareness among teens	Bill to build new high-tech prison
Bill to repair previously retired military vehicles	Bill to increase current police force size by 50%
Department of Recreation	
Bill to start program for volunteer park and roadside cleanups	Bill to purchase land for city parks
Bill to give tax refund for personal gardens and company rooftop gardens	Bill to fund a wildlife reserve
Department of Health	
Bill to start healthy living television and Internet campaign	Bill to start new sanitation program, including more sanitation works and landfill outside of city
Bill to increase fines for companies that don't follow health regulations	Bill to give funding for free long term preventive care

bill ***(n.):*** proposal for a law

Discussion **Questions**

1 Do you usually follow through with self-commitments (diet routine, etc.), or do you often back out halfway through? Why do you think this is?

2 How important is it to **hold someone accountable** when they don't fulfill their commitments?

3 If you could be free of any one of your obligations, which one would you choose and why?

4 Who is responsible for taking care of...

- ...the poor?
- ...the environment?
- ...the elderly?

5 What **chores** around the house are your responsibilities?

- How does your family decide who does various chores around the house?
- If you could have a robot to do one of your chores, what would you choose for it to do?

6 Is there anyone who seems to place too many responsibilities on you? How does this make you feel?

- Have you ever had a really heavy responsibility?
- If you could have a robot to do one of your chores, what would you choose for it to do?

7 How involved should governments be in people's lives?

- How should we hold criminals accountable for their actions?
- Are criminals ever not responsible for their crimes?

UNIT 3 REVIEW

How well can you use:

☐ Be supposed to and be expected to?

What do you need to study more?

back out ***(phrasal v.)*****:** withdraw from a previous commitment
chore ***(n.)*****:** household task
heavy responsibility ***(idiom)*****:** very important responsibility
hold someone accountable ***(idiom)*****:** to consider someone responsible

Activity :Making Excuses

Choose a box and request that thing from your group. Everyone must give a unique excuse.

Alternate Rule: If you can't come up with a response (or it's an illogical response), you are "out". Continue until there is a winner.

Example: Scratch my back.

A: *I'm sorry, I can't. I just did my nails.*

B: *I wish I could, but I'm actually allergic to backs.*

C: *I would love to, but I am wearing oven mitts.*

D: *I think my girlfriend would get jealous!*

EMPLOYEE PERFORMANCE EVALUATION

ABC Efficiency Experts:
Developing Company Efficiency Since 1975!

TOP SECRET

Employee: Richard

Strengths:	Areas for Improvement:
• Well-liked by colleagues • Strong verbal communicator • Able to successfully meet management deadlines	• Tends to work less efficiently than other colleagues • Has trouble focusing on work in a busy office environment

Overall Comments and Suggestions for Improvement:

Richard is a sociable, likeable staff member who communicates effectively with his coworkers and makes a positive contribution to the office environment. He is an excellent team player and takes the time to check in regularly with colleagues. If he wishes to improve his working style, Richard should strive to focus more intently on his work and use his time more wisely. When Richard stops working to check in with coworkers, he often spends much more time than necessary discussing topics unrelated to work. While at his desk, Richard procrastinates at times by looking at social networking sites and online newspapers.

Richard is an excellent employee and an asset to the company. In order to improve his productivity, he should:

- Try to set a few 10-minute breaks every day. During this time, he can talk to coworkers, go for a short walk, drink some coffee or tea, and rest his mind. These breaks should leave him refreshed and ready to go back to work quickly when break time is over.
- Block non-work-related websites, such as social networking sites, from his computer. These sites can be accessed at home, and do not need to be used at work.

A. Discussion

1. What are some adjectives that you would use to describe yourself as an employee or student? Explain your choices.
2. Think about the way you work as an employee or student. What kind of performance evaluation would you give yourself? Talk about strengths and possible suggestions for improvement.

B. Writing

Imagine that you are applying for a job or university program that interests you. Write a paragraph describing why you would be a good employee or student.

04 Sticky Situations

Dilemmas and Conditions

Objectives:

/ Discuss stipulating conditions
/ Listen to a conversation about a dilemma

WARM UP

Look at the pairs below. If you had to choose between the two options, which would you choose?

1.	☐ Chocolate-bacon ice cream	☐ Vanilla-squid ice cream
2.	☐ Lukewarm coffee	☐ Burning hot tea
3.	☐ Unemployed friend's advice	☐ Workaholic uncle's advice
4.	☐ Empty bus in traffic jam	☐ Crowded subway on hot day
5.	☐ 5-hour long documentary	☐ Foreign film with no subtitles
6.	☐ Super fat cat	☐ Really ugly dog
7.	☐ Cheap and stylish, but poor quality	☐ Expensive and ugly, but high quality

Which of these decisions were difficult for you?
Which of these decisions were easy?

IDIOMS

- **Between a rock and a hard place**
  I promised my boyfriend months ago I'd go to the concert, but Julie I have an important project to finish. I'm really *between a rock and a hard place*.
- **Weigh options**
  It's a difficult decision. Before going any further you should *weigh your options* carefully.

PHRASAL VERBS

- **Get out of**
  This is a terrible dilemma. I'm not sure how to *get out of* this without losing money.
- **Work through**
  It was a difficult decision to make, but we *worked through* it and made the right choice.

COLLOCATIONS

- **A no-win situation**
  I can't tell the truth and I shouldn't lie. This is really a *no-win situation*.
- **Whatever (someone) does**
  Whatever I do, someone is going to get hurt.

LESSON 1

A. No Strings Attached

Language Point : Stipulating Conditions

The expressions *Even if* and *Unless* are used to say that a particular condition changes the outcome or should be ignored.

▸ *If your ex-boyfriend is at the party, will you still go?*

Even if - the condition doesn't matter. The result is the same.

▸ *I'll go to the party even if my ex-boyfriend is there. I don't care.*

Unless - the condition does matter. The result would change.

I'll go the party unless my ex-boyfriend is there. I hate that guy.

Look at the questions below and discuss what you would do in the following situations.

What would you do if...

...you asked a woman when she was going to have her baby, and it turned out she was just overweight?

Oh, I would apologize! That's terrible.

What if...

- She insulted your face in response?
  I would apologize even if she insulted me because...
- She was your sister?
  *I would apologize **even if** she's my sister because...*
- She was wearing a shirt saying, "Baby On Board!"?
  *Oh. I would apologize **unless** she was wearing a ridiculous t-shirt.*

stipulation ***(n.)*:** a demand for something

What would you do if...

1 ...you could make a sequel to any movie?

What if...

- The actors in the movie could never be in another movie again?
- You could only watch the movie on a 2G phone?
- They would make five more sequels, but they would all be terrible?

2 ...you were offered a free week at a luxury hotel?

What if...

- You had to be in your room by 7pm?
- Your room was haunted?
- You had to share the room with someone you hated?

3 ...you ripped your pants in the middle of a blind date?

What if...

- You and your date were really **hitting it off**?
- Your date was really boring?
- You forgot to wear underwear?

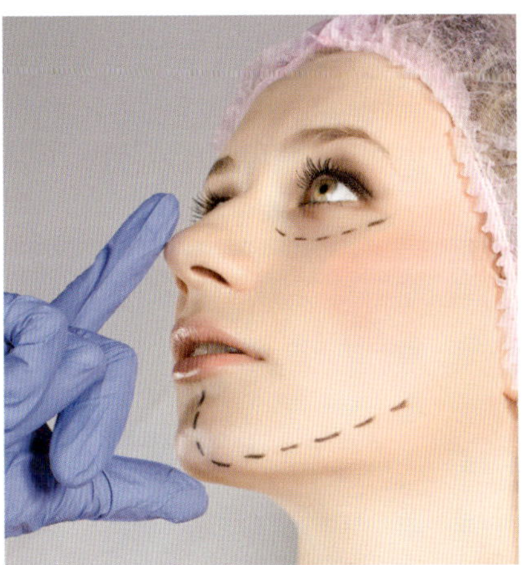

4 ...you could have unlimited free cosmetic surgery?

What if...

- Everyone knew that you had the surgery?
- You weren't allowed to use anesthesia?
- You lost your sense of touch?

5 ...you were parking your car and accidentally bumped into an empty car?

What if...

- No one were around to see it?
- There was a CCTV camera nearby?
- You were borrowing your friend's car?

6 ...they made a super-expensive pill that gives the ability to speak English perfectly for a week?

What if...

- No one could understand you when you spoke in your native language?
- It made you shrink 20 centimeters?
- You were able to get a free year's supply?

7 ...you could be invisible for a day?

What if...

- Everyone else would be invisible too?
- Anything you ate or drank during the day would not turn invisible?
- There's a chance you might become invisible for the rest of your life?

8 ...you were offered a job making $200,000 a year in Antarctica?

What if...

- There were a minimum five year contract?
- You would have no contact with other people?
- At the end of the contract, you got a penguin as a pet?

anesthesia ***(n.):*** medically induced insensitivity to pain
hit it off ***(phrasal v.):*** to get along well with someone else

B. Only If I Have To

Language Point : Even if vs. Only if

Even if expresses that a stipulation doesn't matter,

▸ ***Even if** you think he's cheating, don't tell.*

Only if expresses that something can happen only under a specific condition.

▸ *Tell her **only if** you think he's cheating.*

Pre-listening

Lisa's friends Tom and Tami have been dating for a year. Lisa just saw Tom at the movies with another girl.

- Can two people go to the movies together only if they are a couple? Why or why not?
- Would you let your significant other go to the movies with a member of the opposite sex? Why or why not?

Listening 

TRACK 8-9

Circle which conditions Susan says Lisa should tell Tami about what she saw.

Only if Lisa knows the facts about the situation.

Only if Lisa has talked to Tom first.

Only if Tom was sharing popcorn with the girl.

Only if Tom and the girl seemed "friendly".

Post-listening

1. If you were Lisa, would you tell Tami only if you were sure about what happened, or would you tell her no matter what? Why?

2. Under what condition will you...

> **Example:** ...eat fifty eggs?
>
> **A:** *I'll eat fifty eggs only if you offer me $1000 dollars.*

1 ...give your whole life savings to a friend?

2 ...smash a smart phone on the ground?

3 ...go to work with no pants on?

4 ...pull an all-nighter?

5 ...drink four liters of milk in an hour?

6 ...sing a solo in front of 500 people?

7 ...work for free?

8 ...stop eating your favorite food forever?

C. Pickles

• Unlikely situations

Identify the dilemma in each situation then discuss the right and wrong way to handle each situation.

Example:

You were asked to give a speech about bacon, so you've written an amazing speech. Seconds before you are about to go on stage, you realize it's a vegetarian convention! Thousands of people are waiting to hear your speech.

A: *The wrong thing to do would be to cancel the speech and leave the audience waiting. You should cancel a speech only if you absolutely can't speak.*

B: *Even if you feel unprepared, I think giving the speech is the right thing to do. If I were the speaker, I would give the speech but replace the word "bacon" with "broccoli".*

1 You have been worrying about money lately. You are taking a bus downtown when you notice a wallet that was left on the seat. You look inside the wallet and there is identification, a credit card, and some cash.

2 The final selection for the job you really want is between you and your friend. You just found out that your friend exaggerated a lot about their qualifications and experience.

3 You just found out that a good friend of yours used to date the person you are interested in.

4 Your friends have dared you to spend the night alone in a house that is supposedly haunted. The house is in the middle of the woods and there is no electricity or running water. The nearest neighbors live twenty kilometers away. All you can bring is a flashlight.

5 You just got a job as a chef in a busy restaurant and you accidently drop a customer's steak on the dirty kitchen floor. The customer has already complained about the slow service.

6 You find out that the person you are in love with will be leaving forever in six months. Do you enjoy the time or break it off immediately?

7 You die (peacefully) and are given a choice between finding out what, if anything, happens after death or wandering the Earth forever as a ghost.

8 Your boyfriend or girlfriend owns a hair salon and has given you a really bad haircut.

9 You are on a road trip in the middle of winter and your car breaks down in a small town with only two hotels. Your car will not be repaired until the morning. At one hotel, there is no running water. At the other hotel, there is no heat.

10 You are at your friends' place for dinner and they are serving liver and onions. Whenever you eat liver and onions, you get sick.

11 You discover that there was a mix up at the hospital, and your beautiful one-year-old child is not yours.

Discussion **Questions**

1 When was the last time you were **between a rock and a hard place**?

- ▶ What was the situation?
- ▶ How did you **get out of it**?

2 What was an embarrassing moment you have had in your life?

- ▶ What did you do after you realized you had embarrassed yourself?

3 Do you usually admit to being in a difficult situation, or do you try to pretend everything is okay?

- ▶ Why do you think this is?
- ▶ If you need help, who do you usually ask?

4 Have you ever been in a **no-win situation** when you were…

- ▶ …in school?
- ▶ …at work?
- ▶ …in the army?
- ▶ …with your parents?
- ▶ …with your friends?

5 What valuable things can be learned from difficult decisions?

6 How would you end an unpleasant conversation with someone you didn't know?

- ▶ What do you do in social situations that become uncomfortable?
- ▶ Is it better to suffer through a situation and not be rude or risk being rude and walk away?

between a rock and a hard place ***(idiom)*****:** a difficult situation
get out of ***(phrasal v.)*****:** to avoid doing something
no-win situation ***(n.)*****:** a situation with no good outcome possible

LESSON 2

>> WARM UP

Objectives:

/ Discuss resolutions for sticky situations

You tried to bake a cake for your friend, but realized after baking the cake you used salt instead of sugar. Now, the cake is salty and your friend's birthday party starts in 30 minutes!

> What can you do? Think of possible solutions to the problem.

> Does your solution change under any of the following conditions?

What if...

- ...all of the cakes on sale at the bakery are strawberry flavored, and you know that your friend hates strawberries?
- ...you have been promising to bake a cake for months, and you know that your friend will be disappointed if you don't bring one?
- ...you have no sugar at home?

A. Weighing Your Options

Example:

If Joe quits his job, a pro is that he'll have more time to work on job applications.

Choices in life are never easy. Discuss what the person could do, and talk about the pros and cons of each situation.

On one hand...	...but on the other hand...
1 Joe is short on money and needs a job that pays more.	1 He is so busy at his current job that he hasn't had time to apply for new jobs.
2 Tino wants to study abroad.	2 He has a high paying job in his home country.
3 Alex can't afford an apartment with a garage for his car.	3 His car keeps getting **vandalized** while parked on the street and he can't afford the repairs.
4 Farah wants to buy a house next to a big open space.	4 People keep dumping trash there.
5 Jim wants to get a master's degree.	5 He needs to work to support his family.
6 Since getting married, Rocky has gained weight.	6 He loves watching TV and eating snacks with his spouse.
7 John wants to move out to get away from an annoying roommate.	7 His landlord claims that he can't leave until he pays for damages to the apartment.

vandalize *(v.)*: to destroy another's property without permission

B. Needs vs. Wants

PART 1 ● Look at the list of items below.

- Which items do you feel you simply want?
- Which items do you feel you need?
  Why you would not be able to live without them?

Example: Stove

I wouldn't be able to live without a stove because I use it to prepare all of my meals. Without a stove, I would have nothing to eat.

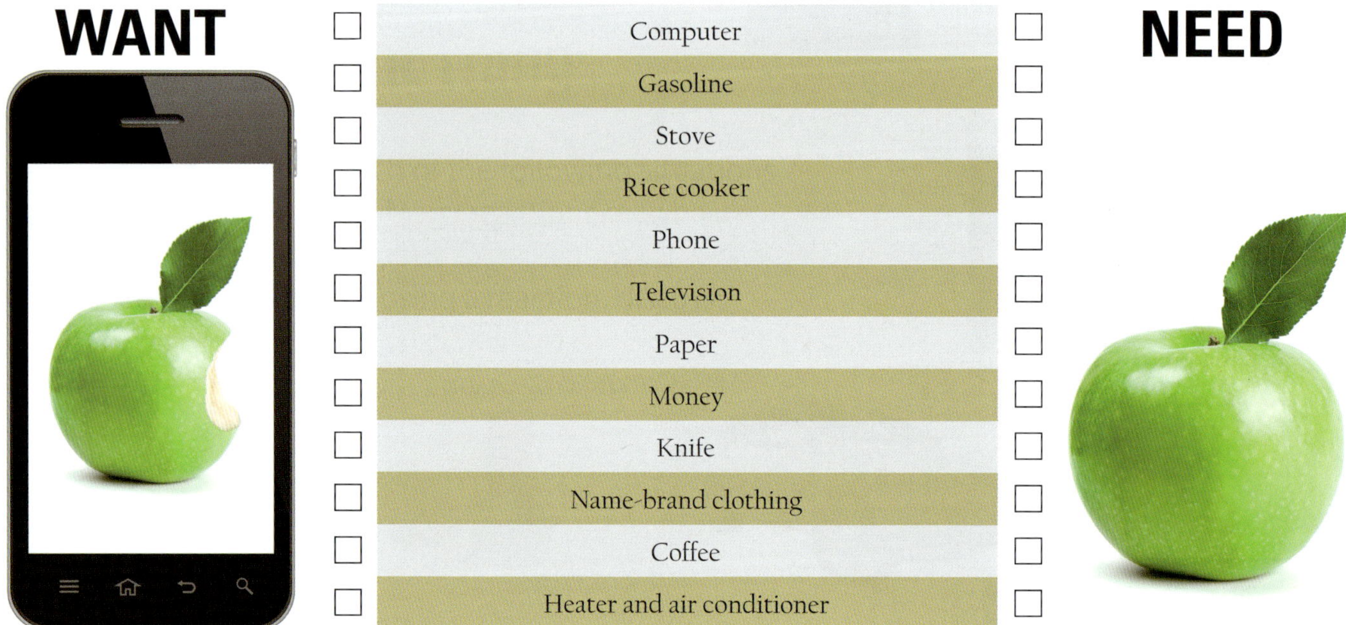

WANT		NEED
☐	Computer	☐
☐	Gasoline	☐
☐	Stove	☐
☐	Rice cooker	☐
☐	Phone	☐
☐	Television	☐
☐	Paper	☐
☐	Money	☐
☐	Knife	☐
☐	Name-brand clothing	☐
☐	Coffee	☐
☐	Heater and air conditioner	☐

PART 2 ● Imagine that you live in a world where the items above do not exist. How could you adapt to do the following activities?

Example: Stay awake.

A: *How would you stay awake if coffee no longer existed?*

B: *I would invent a machine that administers an electric shock every few minutes to keep me awake.*

- Prepare a meal (No stove, rice cooker, or knife)
- Travel 1,000 kilometers (No gasoline)
- Entertain yourself on a rainy afternoon (No computer, phone, television, or money)
- Go on a date (No gasoline, phone, or money)
- Plan a summertime get-together (No computer, stove, rice cooker, phone, knife, or heater and air conditioner)
- Contact a friend who lives 20 kilometers away (No computer, phone, or paper)
- Study for a test (No computer, phone, or paper)

C. Go With the Flow

Guide your partner through the activity, giving them options from the chart and asking follow up questions.

Example:

You hear about a contest for free concert tickets. Do you...

A: *You hear about a contest for free concert tickets! Do you sign up online or call the radio station?*

Sign up online? or **Call the radio station?**

Make a choice and give a reason for your choice.

B: *Hmm...I would call the radio station.*

A: *Really? Why would you do that?*

B: *Because I don't trust signing up for contests online. They're just trying to cheat you.*

You receive a call from the station asking you to...

The radio station says you can have the tickets if you...

Cluck like a chicken. or Bark like a dog. or Croak like frog. or Moo like a cow.

If the box is yellow, act out the situation.

You won free tickets to a concert! Do you...

venue *(n.)*: a place where an event is held

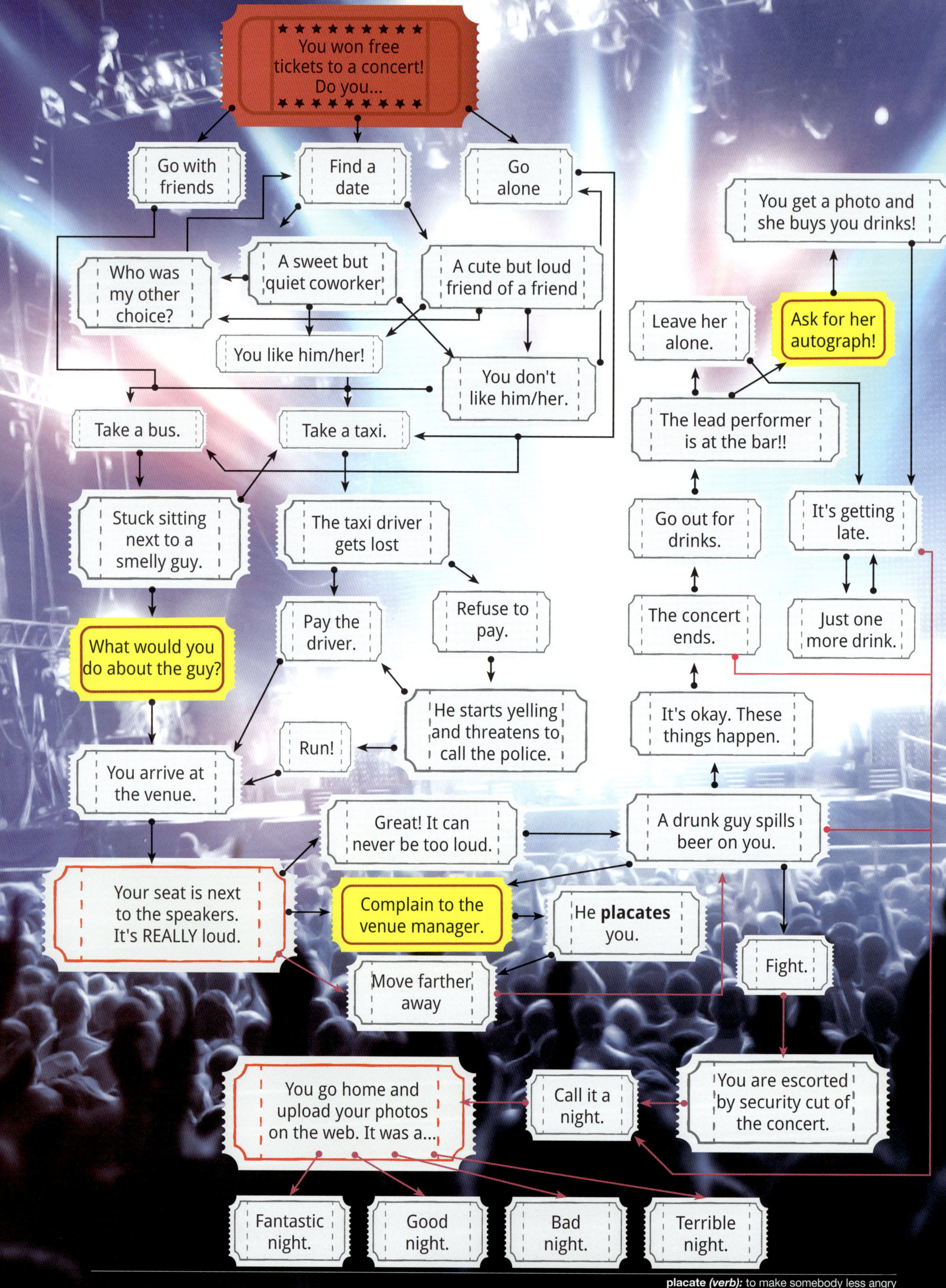

placate ***(verb):*** to make somebody less angry

Discussion **Questions**

1 When you are in a fix, who do you usually turn to for advice? Why?

▶ How do you **weigh** your **options**?

2 Are you the kind of person who tries to please everyone?

▶ Do you think it is possible to keep everyone happy? Why or why not?

3 Do you think that there is a way out of almost every situation, or are there certain situations where whatever you do will have a bad result?

4 Have you ever refused to get involved in another person's problem? Why?

▶ Would you consider yourself good at helping others **work through** their dilemmas?

5 Would you risk your life to save another person? Why or why not?

▶ Would you jump into a river to save a drowning animal?

6 In what situations is it okay to tell a lie?

▶ Is it better to always tell the truth no matter what the outcome might be?

7 Is stealing always wrong?

▶ When might it be okay to steal?

▶ If someone is stealing to feed their family, is it still wrong?

UNIT 4 REVIEW

How well can you use:

☐ Even if, only if, and unless?

☐ On one hand and on the other hand?

What do you need to study more?

fix ***(n.)***: a difficult situation
weigh options (*idiom*): examine pros and cons
work through *(phrasal v.)*: to persevere

Activity : Helping Hand

In your new two-seater car, you are driving down the street in the middle of a terrible thunderstorm. You see a bus stop, and there are three people stuck out in the bad weather. There are no buses anywhere nearby.

As you get closer, you see the three people are:

- A friend
- A very old woman
- An attractive member of the opposite sex

1. What is your first response to the situation? What would you do?
2. Consider some of the following alternatives to the situation below. Which ones would affect your decision and why? Also consider what to do if several of these were true at the same time.

What if your friend...

- ...is currently trying to get you a really good job?
- ...stole your ex-boyfriend/girlfriend?
- ...is really drunk?

What if the old woman...

- ...looks very sick?
- ...looks very angry?
- ...is blind?

What if the member of the opposite sex were...

- ...is the man/woman of your dreams?
- ...is crying?
- ...is ignoring you and chatting on their phone?

Lisa
So...saw someone (not going to say who) at the movies tonight looking pretty cozy with someone who is NOT their significant other. I'm friends both with the person at the movie theater AND the significant other. Ummm....what am I supposed to do?

Tami
Awkward! I would say just keep your lips zipped and see what happens, even if it makes you feel awkward. Maybe the person at the movie theater wasn't who you thought it was.

Tom
Oh shoot! Definitely tell the significant other, even if you feel weird ratting someone out.

Richard
Hi Lisa! Your mother told me that you saw your friend Tom at the movie theater with a girl you didn't know. I'm sorry to see my daughter in such a sticky situation.

Tom
OMG, Lisa, I just read the last post from your dad...is this update about me???

Bob
Lisa, your dad just told everyone who this post is about...and it's about Tom, who just commented!!! AWKWARD! :/

Lisa
Ummm...

Tami
Lisa! Why did you post this instead of just talking to Tom??? Tom was at the movies with his COUSIN! He wasn't on a date with anyone!

Tom
Yeah, I was at the movies with my cousin! You should have just talked to us and I would have introduced you.

Lisa
Ugh...I'm sorry, you guys. I definitely should have talked to Tom instead of posting this all over MyFaceWorld. This post and all of the comments are SO embarrassing! Not just for me, but for Tom and Tami as well.

Tom
It's okay...just talk to me next time. Also...could you please delete this update?

Lisa
Yep, deleting it now.

A. Discussion

1. Why was this post embarrassing for Lisa, Tom, and Tami?
2. What are the pros and cons of posting about personal situations on a public social networking site? Would you ever ask for advice on a personal matter via a social networking site?

B. Writing

Write an email describing a time when you experienced an embarrassing moment. Why was the situation embarrassing? What did you do to save face?

05
Shop Til You Drop

Shopping and Preferences

Objectives:
- Describe products
- Listen to a story about shopping for cell phones

WARM UP

1. Where is the best place to buy...
2. What is your favorite kind or brand of...

- Coffee?
- Cosmetics?
- Cell Phone?
- Toys
- Car?
- Fashion accessories?
- Candy?
- Clothing?

IDIOMS

- **Window shopping**
  I don't have any money, so I can only go *window shopping*.
- **Corner the market**
  They were really able to *corner the market*. Nobody buys anything else.

PHRASAL VERBS

- **Pick out**
  My mom told me I can *pick out* a new jacket at the department store.
- **Buy into**
  I would never *buy into* the claims they make about their product.

COLLOCATIONS

- **Shopping spree**
  I went on a bit of a *shopping spree* last weekend, and now I'm broke.
- **Marketing strategy**
  Our *marketing strategy* is to target the youth market with celebrity endorsements.

Tongue Twister

Sarah saw a shot-silk sash shop
full of shot-silk sashes
as the sunshine shone
on the side of the shot-silk sash shop.

LESSON 1

A. Fashions Fade, Style is Eternal

Language Point : Describing Objects in Detail - Adjective Order

Determiner	Opinion	Size	Age	Shape	Color	Origin	Material	Noun
A	smelly		old		brown			boot
The		huge		baggy			wool	sweater
My	pretty					Japanese	silk	kimono
A pair of		snug	vintage					gloves

◇ Note: We rarely use more than three adjectives when describing an object.

PART 1 ● Take a peek into the family's closet and describe what you find.

> For each type of clothing, discuss what is and isn't fashionable.

> Choose one item from each section to develop an outfit.

> Where could someone go in the outfit you chose?

PART 2 ●

1. What would you wear if you were planning on going...
   > shopping with friends?
   > to a job interview?
   > to a costume party?
2. Describe in full sentences what your partner is wearing using two to three adjectives before each item. Pay attention to the order of the adjectives.

baggy *(adj.)*: hanging loosely
snug *(adj.)*: fitting tightly

B. London Calling

Pre-listening

1. How much did you pay for your cell phone?
   - ▶ Do you think you got a good deal?
   - ▶ How much is too much to pay for a cell phone?

2. What's the oldest thing you own?
   - ▶ Did you pay for it yourself?
   - ▶ How much did you pay for it?
   - ▶ How often do you use it?

Listening  *TRACK 10-11*

Grandpa Charles and Jack are shopping for cell phones. While listening, fill in the blanks with the prices of the different phones.

Grandpa's first phone

THE E-BRICK

Cost: $300

Monthly service: $20

Grandpa's Choices

THE FUSS-FREE 1000

Cost w/contract: __________

Cost w/o contract: __________

Grandpa's Choices

THE I-UNIVERSE IIIX

Cost w/contract: __________

Monthly service: __________

Post-listening

1. Which phone on the left would you choose? Why?
2. Take turns with a partner being the Buyer and the Seller.

Seller

- Think of something you own that you think is valuable: ____________
- Think of how much you would be willing to sell it for, but don't say the price.
- Tell the people in your group you have ________ for sale.
- If people offer you less money than you would sell the item for, argue for why you think it is worth what you want.

Buyer

- Offer a price for the item the other person is selling based on what you think it is worth.
- Debate the price and give reasons why you think the item is only worth the price you've offerered.

C. Don't Count Your Chickens

Choose three investment suggestions from each situation below. Explain why you would choose that investment. You and your partner are…

Example: A newlywed couple

A: *I suggest we buy a new car because we need to plan for a family.*

B: *Come on! I recommend we put that money into insurance policies to be safe.*

1. A newlywed couple

- House
- New car
- Future children's college education
- Jet skis
- Vacation condo
- Insurance (life, medical, and homeowner's insurance)

2. Co-owners of a trendy internet cafe

- State-of-the-art computer equipment
- Renovations (trendier interior design)
- Advertising in the local newspaper
- Turn cafe into a chain and open locations worldwide
- State-of-the-art espresso machine Arcade games

3. Recent graduates of a business administration program

- New cell phone
- Professional attire
- New car
- Apartment downtown
- Laptop computer
- Savings plan for graduate school

4. A recently retired couple

- Yacht
- Grandchildren's education
- Annual tropical vacations
- Convertible sports car
- Luxurious seaside condo
- Medical insurance

5. Co-founders of a small charity group

- Poor children in Africa
- Local homeless people
- Sustainable farming in poor Asian nations
- Bigger, more comfortable office with state-of-the-art equipment
- Hiring a celebrity as a spokesperson for the charity
- Advertising campaign to attract donors

6. CEO and Vice President of a large corporation

- Golf course
- Local charity groups
- Expanding into foreign markets
- Perks for high-level executives (golf trips, company cars, etc.)
- Employee salary increase and benefits package
- Employee team building activities to improve morale

attire *(n.):* clothing
morale *(n.):* level of confidence
perk *(n.):* additional benefit

Discussion Questions

1 What things are currently in fashion that you like?

▶ What is currently out of fashion that you used to wear?

▶ What fashion fad do you think should go out of style?

2 Is a person's fashion sense a good indicator of their personality?

▶ Do people dress the way they feel?

▶ What color or style do you think really **suits you?**

3 How important are name brand or designer clothes to you?

▶ Are they worth the high prices?

4 What is your opinion of knock-off designer brands that are sold for a fraction of the price of the real thing?

▶ Are you good at **picking out** the differences between a fake and a real item?

5 Have you ever been on a **shopping spree** or bought something impulsively and later regretted it?

▶ What did you buy? Do you still have it?

6 In your opinion, which investments are safe? Why?

▶ Which investments are dangerous?

7 Is it better to save money throughout your life or use money to enjoy your time? Why do you think so?

▶ How should people create a balance between the two?

8 Aside from money, people also invest time. What are good investments of your time?

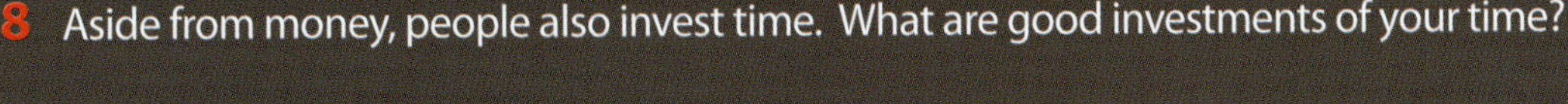

pick out *(phrasal verb):* choose something
shopping spree *(n.):* a shopping trip in which a lot of things are purchased
suit *(verb):* to be the right thing for someone

LESSON 2

>> WARM UP

Objectives:
/ Expand descriptive skills
/ Discuss marketing strategies

Trendy or Tacky?

- What are your thoughts on the fashion styles below?
- What items would you wear?
- What would you never wear?

A. Information Overload

Language Point : Describing Feelings

When describing our feelings, we often use an adjective followed by a preposition and a noun or phrase. The preposition and noun/phrase show what caused the feeling.

- *I'm tired of companies that update their product every six months.*
- *I'm tired of shopping around.*
- *I'm tired of this old dress.*

◇ Note: Certain adjectives connect with certain prepositions. Just like learning when to use an infinitive or a gerund, these collocations can only be learned through practice.

PART 1 ● Ask and answer the questions about consumerism. Make an adjective + preposition combination using one of the prepositions from the list. Once you have used one preposition cross it off the list. Ask a follow up question

1 What are you worried *about* when shopping on the internet?
▶ *How often do you buy things on the internet?*

2 Why is it important to be aware ______all your options when making a big purchase?
▶ ______

3 How often are you satisfied ________ your purchases?
▶ ______

4 What's your favorite brand? What is the brand famous ________?
▶ ______

5 Are you ever amazed _____ the amounts of money people will spend on certain brands?
▶ ______

6 Have you ever been interested _____ starting your own business?
▶ ______

- By
- With
- ~~About~~
- In
- Of
- For

PART 2 ● Use an adjective + preposition combination in your answer and think of a reason why he might feel that way. How does Mr. Man feel about...

... his computer?

...the big sale?

...his new car?

...his cell phone bill?

...his bowling skill?

- Disappointed in
- Proud of
- Angry at
- Content with
- Shocked by

B. Selling Ice to an Inuit

Look at the products below, and think of the best way to market them despite their **shortcomings**. Brainstorm every possible use for each product, then choose one product from each pair. How would you sell it?

Example:

Are you tired of wall decorations that don't do anything? Are you interested in singing animals?

If you answered yes, then the Singing Wall-Mounted Fish has to be the best thing ever invented!

Use it to surprise and entertain your friends! Keep your cat company when you're out!

shortcoming *(n.)*: a failure or flaw

C. It Slices! It Dices!

You're a member of the Spit Polish Advertising & Marketing Company.

> Choose a product from below or make up your own.
> Develop a plan for how to market the product using the chart on the next page.

STEP 1 Develop Your Product.

a. Who is your audience?
b. What need does your product fill?
c. How much will you sell your product for?

STEP 2 Brainstorm Possible Advertisements.

a. Decide how you will advertise your product.
TV Commercial? Radio spot? Website? Viral video?
b. Are there any additional details you can add to improve your concept? A celebrity? A logo? A special promotion? A dance? A jingle?

STEP 3 Develop Your Advertisement.

STEP 4 Present Your Advertisement.

Example:

Product	Dazzler All Purpose Washing Liquid
Audience	Young to middle-aged people with busy lives
Need	Cleaning dishes, washing body, saving time, saving money
Price	$9.99
Advertising method	TV Commercial
Additional	Celebrity endorsement and jingle

Advertising plan presentation: A commercial campaign with a catchy jingle performed by a famous celebrity. Because he has such a busy schedule, he doesn't always have time to wash his dishes. Now he can wash his dishes WHILE having his morning shower. Plates ready to go for breakfast! Jingle: "Hop in to freshen up, then scrub those dishes squeaky clean, every plate and cup!"

Your Product

Product	
Audience	
Need	
Price	
Advertising method	
Additional	

Sample Products or Companies:

Nozz-A-La Cola

Bent's Car Insurance

Mega Fit Health Club, Fitness Package

Sylvia's Skin Clinic, New Super Anti-Aging Skin Cream

Super Champ Dog Food

Hula's Dance Academy, Weekend Dance Camp

ReNewU, Stylist & Makeovers

All-Brite Toothpaste

Steve's Steak Bar, New Menu Item

jingle *(n.):* tune for advertising something
radio spot *(n.):* a radio advertisement
viral *(adj.):* message intended to be spread

Discussion Questions

1 What companies do the best job of marketing their brands?

- ▶ What do you like about their advertising?

2 How much of marketing is lying?

- ▶ How much do you **buy into** the claims companies make about their products?
- ▶ What specific examples can you think of where companies have exaggerated their product?

3 What company do you know of that has **cornered the market** on a product?

- ▶ Who do you think their marketing strategy is aimed at?
- ▶ Which demographic of people is the easiest to get to buy products?

4 What do you think about companies that aim their products toward children?

- ▶ What do you think of the way cigarette or alcohol companies market their products?
- ▶ Should the government be allowed to tell companies how they can market their products?

5 How do products that are from your country measure up in quality to those from abroad?

- ▶ What specific examples can you give of products from your country that are better?
- ▶ How about products that don't measure up?
- ▶ How can local products compete with foreign ones?

6 What do you know about guerilla marketing?

- ▶ Do you think this is a useful way to generate interest in a product?
- ▶ What marketing stunts have you seen in the past? Did the advertising have an effect on you?

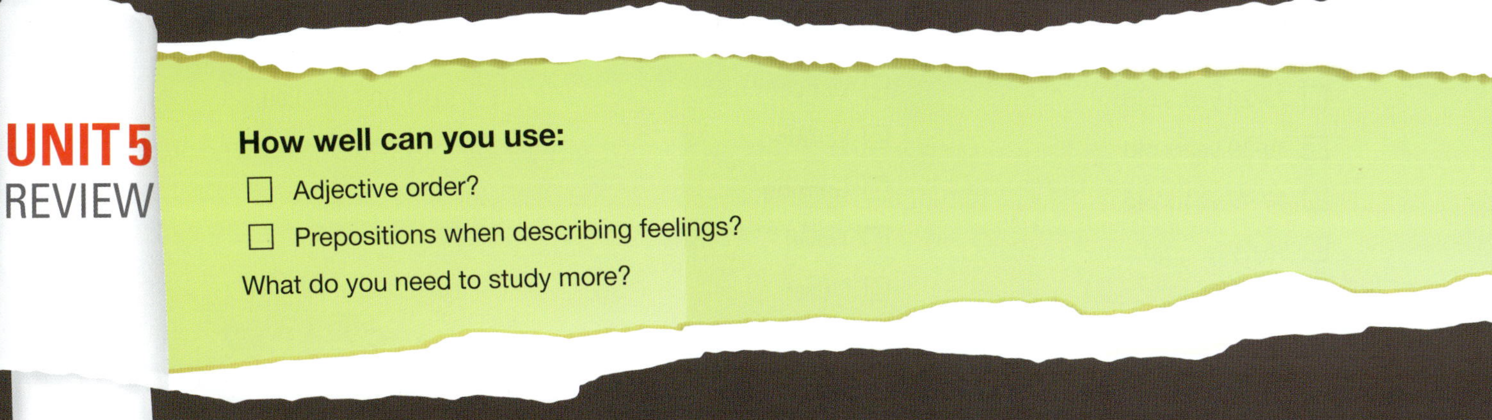

buy into *(phrasal verb):* accept or believe something
corner the market *(idiom):* to become so successful at selling a product that almost no one else sells it

Activity :The Perfect Gift

- Create a profile below, then share the profile with a partner. Your partner must come up with three possible gifts for the person you created and give reasons for their choices.
- Money and gift cards are not allowed.

Example:

A: *I need to buy a gift for a 35-year-old woman who is into sports.*

B: *What's the occasion, and how much do you have to spend?*

A: *It's for her birthday, and I only have about $4.00.*

B: *Uhhh. How about a...*

GENDER

☐ Male
☐ Female

AGE

☐ 0-2 years old
☐ 3-5 years old
☐ 6-12 years old
☐ 13-17 years old
☐ 18-24 years old
☐ 25-29 years old
☐ 30-39 years old
☐ 40-49 years old
☐ 50+ years old

HOBBIES/INTERESTS

☐ Food/cooking
☐ Sports
☐ Clothing/fashion
☐ Cosmetics
☐ Health
☐ Being outdoors
☐ Reading
☐ Television/movies
☐ Dance/music
☐ Painting
☐ Gaming
☐ Travel
☐ Other

OCCASION

☐ Birthday
☐ Anniversary
☐ Retirement
☐ Holiday
☐ Housewarming
☐ Other

BUDGET:

☐ Free - $5.00
☐ $6.00 - $20.00
☐ $21.00 - $50.00
☐ $51.00 - $100.00
☐ $101.00 - $500.00
☐ $501,000 - Money is no object

A. Discussion

1. Which of the apps above sounds the most useful?
   • Which one do you think is the best value?
2. What apps do you use that you find really useful?
   • What do you like about them, and how often do you use them?
3. What do you think about products that are marketed towards a specific age group such as the elderly or children?
   • What examples can you think of that illustrate this?

B. Writing

Think of a new app that would be useful for a certain group of people, and write a short description of it that describes how it is useful.

06
The Art of Conversation

Communication Skills

Objectives:

/ Improve conversational flow

/ Listen to a story about a misunderstanding

WARM UP

Choose the best answer for each step, and say why you think it's the best choice. When starting a conversation with strangers, it's best to...

1 Approach...

A. a large group of people.
B. a couple of people.
C. someone standing alone.

2 Start with...

A. "There's a lot of people here today."
B. "This is a really nice ______________ ."
C. "The weather today is really ______________."

3 Talk about....

A. yourself
B. what the person is wearing or holding
C. what the person does

IDIOMS

- **Talk to a brick wall**
  A conversation with him is like *talking to a brick wall*.
- **Blow it out of proportion**
  She *blew the story a little out of proportion*. I wasn't that drunk, and there was only one clown.

PHRASAL VERBS

- **Strike up**
  I have a lot of difficulty *striking up* conversations with strangers.
- **Talk up**
  I think he spent a lot of time *talking up* the specifics to make himself sound better.

COLLOCATIONS

- **Take forever**
  This bus ride is *taking forever*! At this speed, we won't be there until next year.
- **Conversation piece**
  I love my new bag. It makes a great *conversation piece* whenever I go out.

LESSON 1

A. The Conversationalist

Language Point : Showing that You're Listening

We give quick responses or replies to something that another person has said to show the speaker that we are listening, and to keep the conversation flowing.

Personal Response	
Showing Attention	*- Right.* *- Sure.* *- Uh-huh.*
Showing Interest	*- That's interesting.* *- Is that right?* *- Oh, yeah?*
Showing Surprise	*- You're kidding!* *- Really?* *- I can't believe it!*
Showing Sympathy	*- That's too bad.* *- I'm sorry to hear that.* *- Oh, no!*

A follow-up question can also be a personal response.

A: *I'm going to Hawaii!*
B: *You are? When?*

PART 1 • Read the statement to your partner. Answer the statement with an appropriate response and a follow up question. Try to keep the conversation going as long as you can.

> **Example:** My dog died last night.
> **A:** *My dog died last night.*
> **B:** *I'm sorry to hear that. How old was he?*

1. I won the lottery last night.
2. I broke my finger playing basketball.
3. My birthday is tomorrow.
4. I won't be here because I'm going on vacation.
5. My father was in an accident last night.
6. I really don't like this kind of weather.

PART 2 • Make a statement about one of the topics on the right that is true for you. Read the statement out loud in a group. Every other member of the group must then reply and ask a follow-up question.

> **Example:** Most recent trip
> **A:** *I went on a trip to Kodiak Island.*
> **B:** *That's interesting. Where is that?*
> **A:** *It's off the coast of Alaska.*
> **C:** *You're kidding! Were there bears?*
> **A:** *Yes, everywhere. A bear chased me and I dropped my camera.*
> **B:** *Oh no! Were you really scared?*

- Most recent trip
- Favorite food
- Best class in school
- A really good movie
- Something sad
- An interesting fact
- An injury or illness
- Dream job

B. Conversation Breakdown

Language Point : Sentence Stress to Clear Up a Misunderstanding

Often in conversation, speakers will stress a particular word in a sentence. By placing stress on one word, you can tell someone that they have misunderstood you.

A: *I want a* ***large*** *latte.* **B**: *Oh right. You want a* ***large****, not a small latte.*

A: *I want a large* ***latte****.* **B**: *Really? I thought you said Americano.*

A: *I want* ***a*** *large latte.* **B**: *Okay. Just* ***one****, not two.*

Pre-listening

Match the sentence below to the misunderstanding occurring in the picture.

1. Grandpa Charles: No sorry. I want a **large** pizza.
2. Grandpa Charles: I said I want a large **pizza**.
3. Grandpa Charles: I want **a** large pizza, please.

Listening  *TRACK 12-13*

While listening, match each family member to their complaint.

1. Lisa
2. Martha
3. Richard

a. Wanted peppers
b. Trying to be a vegetarian
c. Thinks that a meat pizza is unhealthy

Post-listening

- Read the sentences below and choose one word in the sentence to stress.
- Clear up the misunderstanding by commenting on the stressed word.

Example:

A: *My friend bought a* ***new*** *sports car.*

B: *Oh I see. Your friend bought a* ***new****, not a* ***used****, car.*

- My friend bought a new sports car.
- How much are the red boots?
- When do you finish work on Friday?
- There are several pieces of cake left in the fridge.
- The best place to eat fish is near the beach.
- I don't hate the green knit scarf.

C. Finding an In

For each of the situations below, start a conversation to break the awkward silence. Decide who will break the ice. Choose a topic from below to begin the conversation. Use the question given or come up with your own.

Example: Sitting on a ski lift

A: *I like your boots. Are they comfortable?*

B: *Thanks. Yeah, they really are. I've been searching for boots that don't kill my feet.*

A: *Really? Me too. Where did you get them?*

B: *I bought them in a store called The Ski Barn in my hometown.*

A: *Oh yeah? Where are you from?*

Tip

A good way to start a conversation is to use a rhetorical question. A rhetorical question is a question that you already know the answer to.

A: *It's really cold here, isn't it?*

B: *Yeah! It's freezing. I should have brought a jacket.*

A: *Do you think the weather will get warmer?*

You are...

1. ...sharing a room in a London hostel with each other.
2. ...starting a job at a large company on the same day.
3. ....introduced by mutual friends at a costume party.
4. ...sitting next to each other on a long train ride to Beijing.
5. ...trapped in an elevator between the 19th and 20th floors.
6. ...standing in line at a tech convention.

Friends *What's the best place to hang out around here?*

TV/Movies *Have you seen the movie ______?*

Traveling *How long have you been here?*

Shopping *Where did you buy your ______?*

Family *Where are you from?*

Cars *What is the best car on the market these days?*

Technology *I see you have a ______. Do you like it?*

Music *Have you heard the new ____ album?*

Current Events *Have you heard about ______?*

Work *What do you do?*

School/Major *What did you study?*

Hobbies *What do you like to do on your day off?*

Sports *What do you think about the ______?*

Past Experiences *Have you ever been to ______?*

Discussion **Questions**

1 Have you ever been in a situation where you wanted to **strike up** a conversation but felt scared to do so?

▶ Where were you?

▶ What could you have done differently?

2 Do you ever have conversations with people sitting next to you on the bus or on an airplane?

▶ Do you enjoy these types of conversations, or do they make you feel uncomfortable?

3 Do you enjoy doing ice breakers at work or in classes, or would you rather simply get to work?

▶ What are the pros and cons of ice breakers?

4 Would you consider yourself to be a talkative person?

▶ When is it appropriate to talk a lot? When is it inappropriate?

5 Have you ever had a conversation with someone where it felt like you were **talking to a brick wall**?

▶ What reasons do we have for miscommunication?

▶ What kind of people do you find it difficult to talk to?

6 What do you own that makes a good **conversation piece**?

▶ When you want to start a conversation with someone, what do you usually remark on? (clothes, sports)

---

conversation piece (*idiom*): something unusual that provokes conversation
strike up (*phrasal v.*): begin a conversation
talk to a brick wall (*idiom*): the person being spoken to does not listen

LESSON 2

>> WARM UP

Objectives:

/ Learn about euphemism, exaggeration, and sentence stress

Which of the questions below would you consider appropriate to discuss with a new acquaintance? Which are inappropriate?

Topic	Appropriate	Inappropriate
What do you think of the weather today?	■	■
Are you single?	■	■
How old are you?	■	■
What is/was your major in university?	■	■
What is your religion?	■	■
What's your biggest regret?	■	■
What is the scariest thing you've ever done?	■	■
What do you think about the president?	■	■
Where's the best place to hang out around here?	■	■

A. Chew Your Words

Language Point : Choosing Your Words

In conversation, speakers sometimes adjust their language to be more gentle or **harsh**.

Gentle

- *I think you might have a little spot on your shirt.*
- *Did you notice that you spilled something on your shirt?*
- *You have something all over your shirt.*
- *You have huge, blue and orange spots all over your shirt!*

Harsh

PART 1 ● Brainstorm some gentle and harsh ways to say the following sentences.

1 "You have a piece of spinach between your teeth."

2 "You are a bad singer."

3 "I didn't like the restaurant."

4 "I never want to see you again."

> **Tip**
> A euphemism is a more delicate, indirect way to say something that would otherwise sound rude or harsh if stated directly.

PART 2 ● Look at the pictures below. Think of a gentle and a harsh way that you could mention each problem. Then, consider possible solutions to each problem.

Tom's bathroom is messy.

Nora is busy.

Jill is carrying too much stuff.

The boss is angry.

Kim looks upset.

The students' class is boring.

harsh ***(adj.)***: difficult to endure

B. A Little Bit Over the Top...

Language Point : Exaggeration

To exaggerate, **embellish** events or moments in the story that make it more interesting.

- Use adjectives that express an extreme idea:

Okay → Good → Amazing   Not great → Bad → Horrible

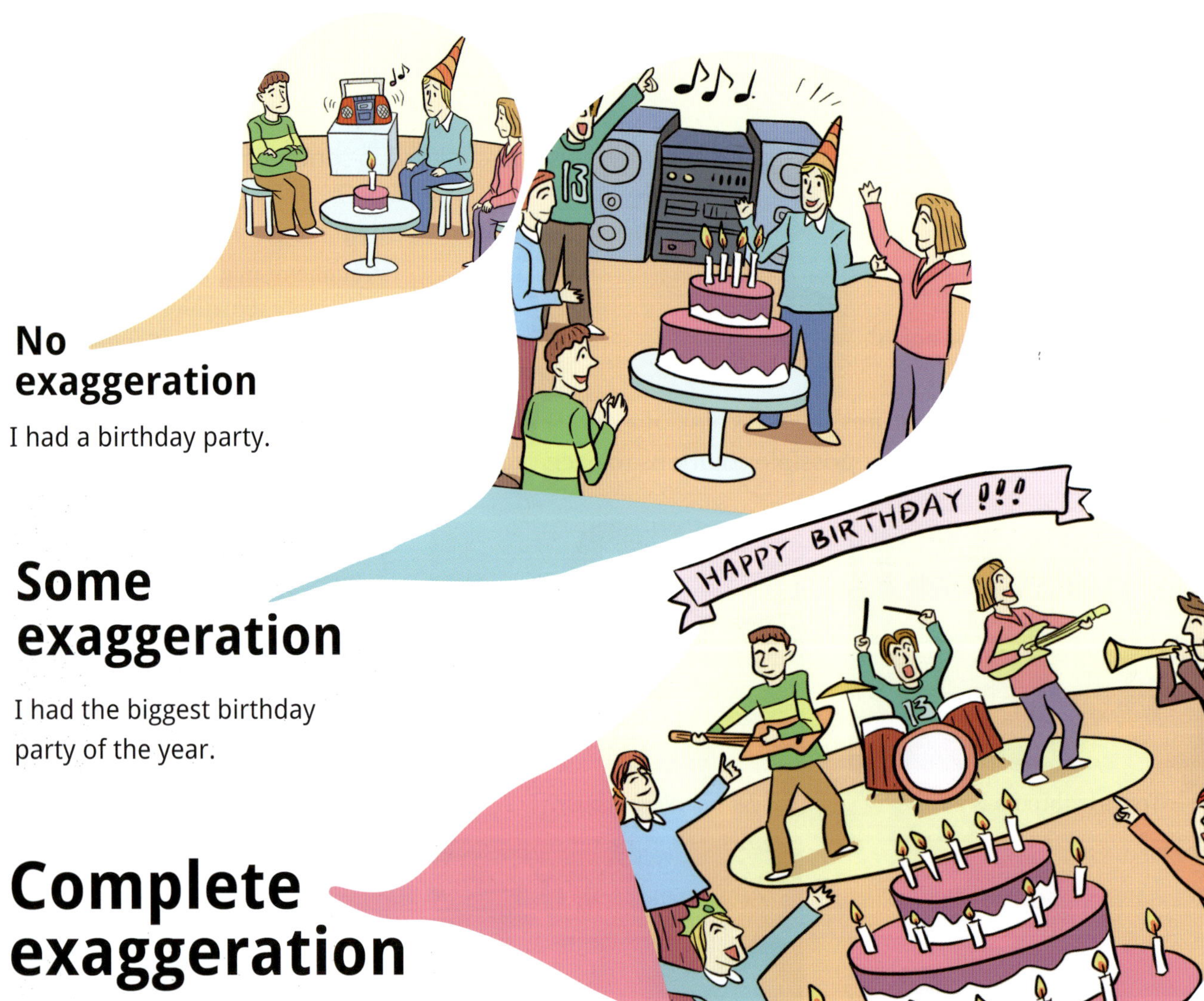

No exaggeration

I had a birthday party.

Some exaggeration

I had the biggest birthday party of the year.

Complete exaggeration

I had the biggest birthday party in the history of the world.

Embellish (*v.*): to make something sound better or worse than it is

PART 1

With a group…

- Ask the question to your group.
- A second person must answer with an exaggerated statement.
- The next person should exaggerate even more.

Example: What did you eat for lunch?

A: *I had a hamburger.*

B: *Oh yeah? I had a huge sandwich.*

C: *Well, I ate a lunch that was bigger than anything else I've eaten in my entire life.*

Questions:

- What did you eat for lunch?
- What did you buy the last time you went shopping?
- How often do you exercise?
- What sports do you enjoy?
- Have you ever seen a celebrity?
- What was the last trip you took?

PART 2 

With a partner…

- Describe what you did last weekend. Give at least three details.
- Your partner(s) must restate what you said, but exaggerate everything.

Example:

A: *So, what did you do last Saturday?*

B: *Well…I didn't really do anything. I woke up late, watched a boring movie, and ate noodles.*

A: *She said she woke up so late that she almost won the world record for sleeping in. Then, she watched a movie that was so boring that it almost made her fall asleep again. After that, she ate an enormous bowl of noodles!*

Tip Lying vs. Exaggerating

It's easy to confuse a lie and an exaggeration. An exaggeration takes a true idea and makes it greater than it actually is for emphasis. Lying is giving a deliberately false statement with the purpose of deceiving others.

C. Exaggeration Evaluation

Tell a true story about yourself using the topics below. Exaggerate about one of the details. See if your partner can guess which one you are exaggerating about.

Example:

A: *Well, I went on my first date when I was really old. I was probably the oldest person on a first date, ever. The guy that I went on a date with was about the same age as me, so he was pretty old too. On the day of the date, the weather was terrible! It was so bad that we could barely even walk outside at all.*

B: *Wait! You're exaggerating about the weather, aren't you?*

A: *I was exaggerating about my age. I wasn't really that old when I went on my first date.*

1. Your first date
- Your age
- The other person's age
- Where

3. Something scary that happened to you
- When
- Where
- What happened

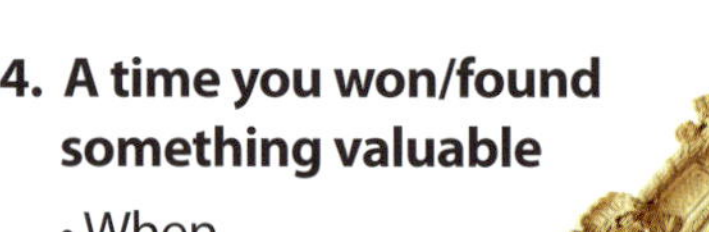

4. A time you won/found something valuable
- When
- What
- Where
- How

2. A time when you were lost
- Who
- Where
- When
- How
- What happened

6. A time when you won a competition
- When
- Where
- Kind of competition
- How you won

5. The number of countries you have visited
- Countries
- When
- Length of visit
- Activities

Discussion **Questions**

1 Have you ever been on a trip that felt like it **took forever**?

▶ How long was the trip really?

2 Do you think it is okay to exaggerate on your resume?

▶ What details do people usually embellish to make themselves look better?

3 Companies often exaggerate about their products and services in order to make more money. What do you think of this practice?

▶ Can you think of an example of a company or product that is advertised to be better than it is?

4 Do you think exaggeration makes a story more interesting, or do you prefer to hear the actual facts?

▶ Which shows can you think of that exaggerate stories to make them more appealing?

5 When couples fight, they tend to **blow things out of proportion**. Why do you think couples tend to make small things bigger than they actually are when fighting?

6 Have you ever had to talk someone up to make them sound better to....

▶ ...your parents? ▶ ...your friends? ▶ ...your boss or coworkers?

7 Why do you think politicians use euphemisms in their language?

8 Can you think of a more euphemistic way to say...

▶ ...war? ▶ ...fat? ▶ ...dead? ▶ ...handicapped? ▶ ...fired? ▶ ...ugly?

UNIT 6 REVIEW

How well can you use:

☐ Appropriate responses during conversation?

☐ Sentence stress?

☐ Euphemism and exaggeration?

What do you need to study more?

took forever (*idiom*): an extremely long time
blow it out of proportion (*idiom*): to overreact to something

Activity : This is a...

1. The leader hands an object or a word to the left. (A pen for example)
2. The leader says, "This is a pen."
3. The person who receives the object must answer by saying, "A what?"
4. The leader replies again, "A pen."
5. The first receiver then passes the object to the next person, saying, "This is a pen."
6. The next receiver replies, "A what?"
7. The word is passed around the entire circle.
8. The leader then passes on another word to the right, following the same procedure.

www. Food online.com

Food online - Restaurant of the week

Popular Pizza People: Just About The Best Pizza EVER!

Rating: 

PNN food lovers will be thrilled to try the new pizza shop that just opened on Main Street: Popular Pizza People. The name is quite a tongue-twister, and the pizza puts a new "twist" on the usual pie.

I went to eat at this restaurant with my family. My wife and I got the "Veritable Veggie" pizza, which included a basil-tomato sauce and three kinds of cheese, along with mushrooms, spinach, onions, olives, peppers, and corn. All of the flavors of the veggies blended perfectly to make a delicious dinner, even without meat.

For the kids, we ordered a simple "Cheesy Tom", which had a basil tomato sauce topped with mozzarella cheese. The pizza wasn't greasy, and the kids finished their pie faster than my wife and I!

The restaurant had a trendy décor, but was very kid-friendly. In our opinion, the only downside was the price of the meal. For one medium and one small pizza, we paid about $35. Despite the prices, I highly recommend this for anyone who knows how to appreciate a good, original pie!

Comments:

Lisa: I KNEW we should have ordered the veggie! My family just got a takeout pizza from Popular Pizza People last night. We had the Popular Pepperoni Pie—it was okay, but I would have loved to go meatless.

Charles: Great review! However, I would recommend the Popular Pepperoni Pie. I picked one up for my family last night and everyone loved it!

Lisa: Grandpa—is that you? I didn't know you used this site!

A. Discussion

1. According to the review, what are some of the pros and cons of Popular Pizza People? After reading the review, would you consider eating at a restaurant like this?
2. How often do you look for recommendations or reviews when deciding where to eat? What are some of your favorite resources for information about good restaurants?

B. Writing

Write a review of a restaurant where you've eaten. Describe the pros and cons of the restaurant and write whether or not you recommend it to others.

07 Escape from Reality

Dreams and Escapes

Objectives:

/ Express skepticism
/ Listen to a story about a dream
/ Interpret dreams and thoughts

WARM UP

1. What are three common things people see in dreams?
   - ______________________
   - ______________________
   - ______________________

   What does it mean to dream about these things?

2. What are three supernatural beings?
   - ______________________
   - ______________________
   - ______________________

   Do you think any of them might actually exist?

IDIOMS

- **In my wildest dreams**
  Even *in my wildest dreams* I never thought I'd see you again.
- **Capture someone's imagination**
  The fantasy *novel captured the world's imagination* and sold millions of copies.

PHRASAL VERBS

- **Dream up**
  I spent last night trying to *dream up* creative things to do at the party.
- **Live out**
  They go to the park and live out their fantasies by dressing in costumes.

COLLOCATIONS

- **A figment of someone's imagination**
  I think the noises you heard last night were *just a figment of your imagination.*
- **Like a dream**
  The trip was *like a dream*. Everything we saw and did was amazing.

TONGUE TWISTER

I wish I were what I was when I wished I were what I am.

A. I Don't Buy It

Language Point : Expressing Skepticism

To be skeptical about...
▸ *I'm skeptical about the existence of ghosts.*

To doubt...
▸ *I doubt that humans can have psychic powers.*

To not buy...
▸ *I don't buy the story of the lake monster.*

PART 1 ● Check whether you think the theories are very likely, likely, or not likely and discuss why you think so. If you think a theory is not likely, express your skepticism.

Example:

A: *I think it's likely that life exists on other planets. I doubt that we are the only life in the universe.*

B: *I'm not sure I buy it. If there were life on other planets, wouldn't we know by now?*

	Very Likely	Likely	Not Likely
1 Eating meat is good for your heath.	☐	☐	☐
2 Studying all night for a test will help you pass.	☐	☐	☐
3 Eating carrots will help you see in the dark.	☐	☐	☐
4 There is a secret society that controls all of the world's leaders.	☐	☐	☐
5 Ghosts are among us.	☐	☐	☐
6 Time travel is possible.	☐	☐	☐
7 Life exists on other planets besides Earth.	☐	☐	☐
8 A person's blood type influences his or her personality.	☐	☐	☐
9 Humans can have psychic powers.	☐	☐	☐
10 Dreams that we have while sleeping can give us messages about our waking life.	☐	☐	☐

- Comparatives and superlatives
- Speculation
- Contrasting using Even though

PART 1

In the images below are some common mythical creatures.

> Discuss who would be better in the situations and why you think so.

> Your partner HAS to disagree - express skepticism and explain why the other choice is more likely.

Example:

Who is more likely to win a race: a genie or a pegasus?

A: *I think it's more likely that the pegasus would win because he has wings, so he can fly!*

B: *Seriously? Genies can grant wishes, so he can just wish himself to the finish line.*

A: *I don't agree with that. He can GRANT wishes, but that doesn't mean he can wish things for himself.*

B: *Says who? Besides, genies can fly too, I think.*

Who would win a cooking competition?

A dragon or a mermaid

Who would win a wrestling match?

The Tooth Fairy or the Easter Bunny

Who would get the highest score on the university entrance exam?

Santa or an alien

Who would be a better blind date?

Medusa or a ghost

Who would be a better president?

A vampire or a werewolf

Who would be more fun on a road trip?

A zombie or Big Foot

psychic *(adjective):* able to see the future or read people's thoughts

Do You Remember: Disagreement

Formal: *I'm afraid I disagree with you.*
Neutral: *I don't agree. / Are you sure about that?*
Informal: *That's ridiculous! / No way!*

B. Lisa Through the Looking Glass

Pre-listening

Some fields of psychology suggest items in our dreams represent things happening in our daily lives. Look at the symbols below. What do you think they represent?

Listening *TRACK 14-15*

Listen to Lisa's story and find out what symbols she sees in her dreams.

What additional symbols from below are mentioned?

__ Paralyzed

__ Trying to move, but not getting anywhere

__ Attic

__ Hair

__ Mirror

__ Games

__ Teeth falling out

__ Being watched

__ Towers

__ Money

Post-listening

PART 1 ● Lisa certainly has vivid dreams!

Look at your list of symbols from Lisa's story, and analyze her experience.

> What kinds of things do you think Lisa is dealing with in her life right now?

> Why do you think so?

Post-listening

PART 2 ● The Dream Interpreter

Step 1

Choose either a recent dream you've had OR Lisa's dream to interpret. If it's your own dream, tell it to your partner in as much detail as you can remember.

> **Example:**
>
> *I have this reoccurring dream where I'm waiting for the bus, but when the bus arrives, the driver is a giant bear!*

Step 2

Put each idea from the dream into one of the categories below. Then discuss the possible meaning of each symbol, and what the symbol might mean.

People	**Things**
Places	**Activities**

> **Example:**
>
> Bear, Thing; Bus stop, Place
>
> **A:** *So maybe the bus stop is your impatience.*
>
> **B:** *I hate waiting. And I am waiting to hear about a new project at work...*

Step 3

Do you think the dream was about:

- Personal Conflict (Self-doubt, guilt, etc.)
- Wish-fulfillment (Travel, romance, etc.)
- Problem Solving (Work problems, social problems, etc.)
- Visions of the future (Warnings, suggestions, etc.)

> **Example:**
>
> **A:** *I don't think I want to meet a bear, so it's not wish-fulfillment. I don't really believe in future vision things. So, it must be some kind of personal conflict.*

Step 4

Now that you've interpreted the dream, is there anything you should change or consider in your day-to-day life? If you chose Lisa's dream, what advice would you give her?

---

attic *(n.)*: open area immediately under the roof of a house
paralyzed *(adjective)*: unable to move

C. The Deepest Meaning

PART 1 ● Imagine that you are having a dream.

1. You wake up in a house. Walk through the rooms.
- What is your house like?
- What kind of things are inside?

2. You walk outside and look at the garden.
- What does the garden look like?
- How does being in the garden make you feel?

3. You leave the garden and start walking through woods. Look at the trees.
- What are the woods like?
- How do you feel while walking through them?
- How long do you walk through the woods?

4. While walking through the woods, look down on the ground. You see a key.
- What does the key look like?
- What do you think you can do with this key?

5. You look up and see an animal.
- What does the animal look like?
- What do you do?

6. After seeing the animal you continue walking. You find a cup sitting on a log.
- What does the cup look like?
- What is it made of ?
- What is inside of it ?

7. At the end of the woods you come to a wall. You cannot go to the other side.
- What does the wall look like?
- Are you afraid of or curious about what is on the other side?
- What do you think is on the other side?

PART 2

Look at the meaning behind the different aspects of your dream and discuss the relevance.

1. **The House** - this symbolizes the idea of yourself and how you want others to see you.
   - What does your house look like?
   - What kinds of things are inside? What do you think they represent?

2. **The Garden** - this symbolizes the way you think about the environment where you live.
   - How do you feel about the environment you live in?
   - Is it positive or negative?

3. **The Woods** - this symbolizes your journey through life and how you see other people.
   - Does your feeling while walking through the woods describe your feeling about life?
   - If the woods represent other people, how do you feel about them?

4. **The Key** - this symbolizes your ambitions for your life.
   - Would you consider yourself an ambitious person? Why or why not?

5. **The Animal** - this symbolizes how you see and deal with your problems.
   - Do you think your problems are big or small?
   - How do you deal with your problems?

6. **The Cup** - this symbolizes your idea of love.
   - What the cup is made of symbolizes the strength of your love. Do you think it's strong?
   - How is what's inside the glass important?
   - What do you think this means about your idea of love?

7. **The Wall and the Other Side** - this symbolizes your feelings about death and the afterlife.
   - How does the way the wall looks relate to your idea of death?
   - Do you believe in life after death?
   - What about having past lives?

---

afterlife *(n.):* the idea of life after death

Discussion Questions

1 What do you think about dream interpretation? Is it real or a superstition?

- What can dreams tell us about our waking life?

2 Do you remember what you dream about?

- Would you like to stop having dreams or have more dreams?
- Why do you think some people remember their dreams and others don't?

3 Have you ever …

- …woken up and believed you were still in your dream?
- …been falling in a dream and just when you were about to hit the ground woken up?
- … woken up from a dream and been unable to move?

4 Do you ever have lucid dreams? In other words, do you ever become aware that you are dreaming and then control the dream?

- Have you ever been in a situation that was exactly like a dream?

5 Do you know anyone who claims to have seen a ghost?

- Why do you think that so many people believe in ghosts?

6 What is the most ridiculous thing people have **dreamt up**?

- Why don't you believe it?

7 What supernatural beings (aliens, vampires, etc.) might exist?

- Why do you think so?
- Which ones are just **figments of our imagination**?

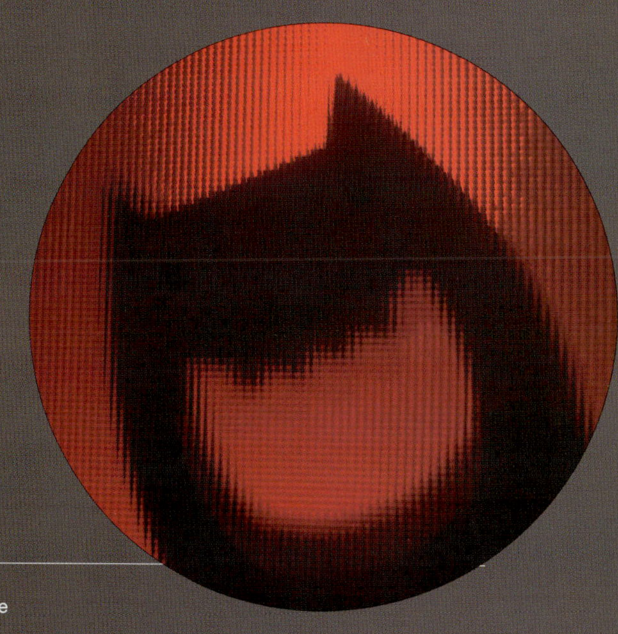

dream up *(phrasal verb)*: invent something
figment of someone's imagination *(idiom)*: something created by the mind that's not really there

LESSON 2

>> WARM UP

Objectives:
/ Practice using the verb *wish*

If you were a genie and could grant people wishes, what three rules would you have?

-
-
-

Keeping your three rules in mind, you are now a genie! Grant your partner three wishes.

A. I Wish My Brother George Were Here

Language Point : Changing Reality with the Verb *Wish*

Making a wish about the past - the past perfect is used to make a wish about the past. What you wanted did not happen.

- *I wish I **had gone** backpacking last summer.*

Making a wish about the present - the simple past is used to make a wish about the present. You want reality to be different.

- *I wish I **spoke** German. -or- I wish I **could** speak German.*

Making wishes about the future - "would" is used if you want something to happen, or you want someone to do something.

- *I wish he **would** come to the party this weekend.*
- *I wish the bus **would** come. It's really cold.*

Tip Although "were" is correct for making wishes about the present, "was" is often used in informal conversation.

Example: *He wishes he **were** alone.*

*He wishes he **was** alone.*

PART 1

What do you wish were different about…

1 …where you live?

2 …your school?

3 …your city

4 …your job?

5 …the weather?

6 …your classroom?

• Modals for speculation

PART 2

Look at the pictures. Make guesses about…

- …what problem each person or group of people might have.
- …what they wish were different right now.
- …what they wish would be different in the future.

Example:

A: *It looks like Twiggy might be waiting for someone to call her and offer her a job.*

B: *She wishes she were out with her friends.*

C: *She probably wishes the phone would ring.*

1. Madeleine and her parents have been arguing.

2. Max has been waiting a long time.

3. Biff and Lisa have been shopping for hours.

4. Captain Kid has been training in order to face his enemy.

5. Jade has been on a diet.

6. Tania has been waiting for the bus for over an hour.

B. The Escapist

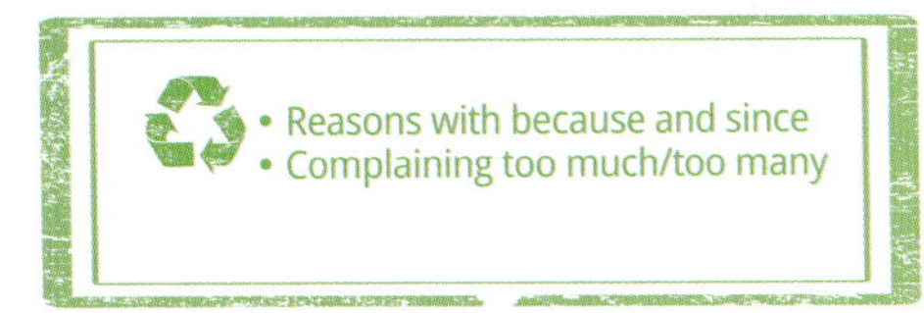

PART 1 ● Put the following activities into the chart below based on what YOU think is a healthy, harmless, or dangerous means of escape.

- What makes this escape healthy?
- How often do you do this?

- What makes this escape harmless?
- Can it become dangerous?

- Why do you think this so dangerous?
- Have you ever tried escaping in this way?

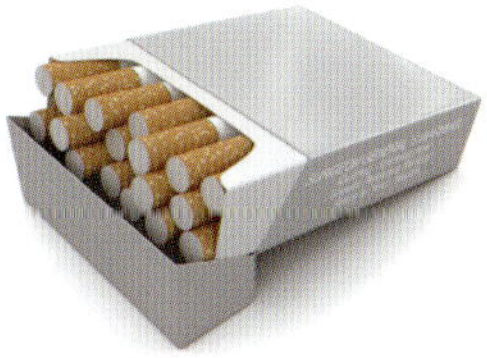

01 Smoking

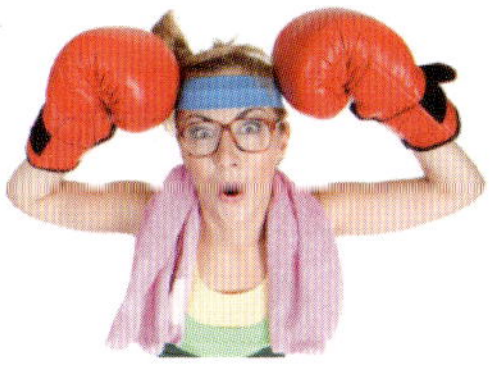

02 Exercising

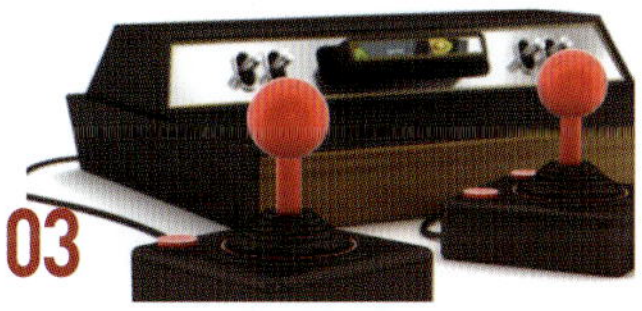

03 Playing games

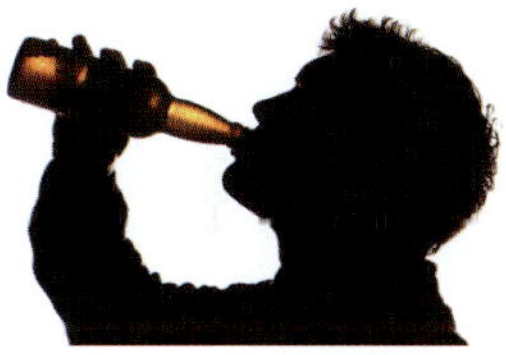

04 Drinking Alcohol

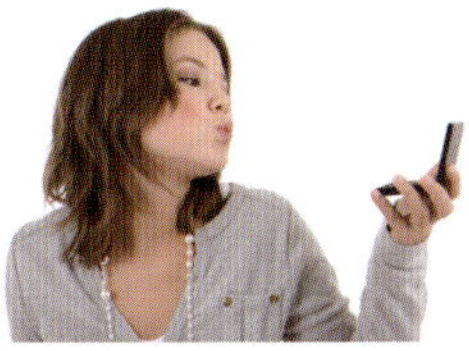

05 Grooming

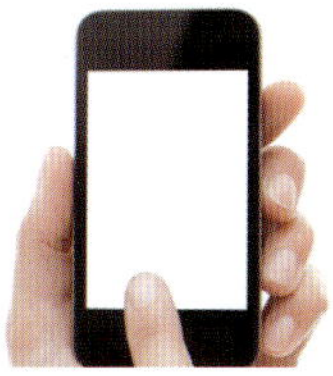

06 Using smart phones

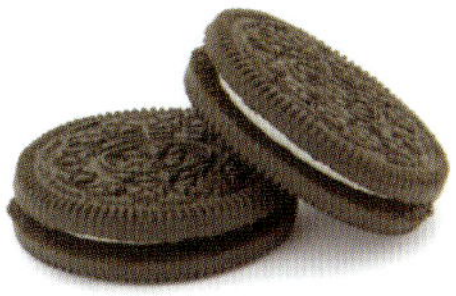

07 Snacking

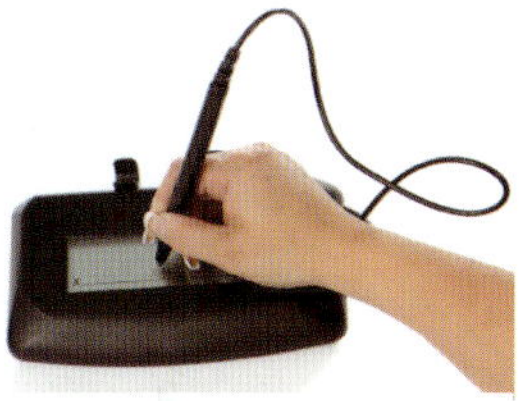

08 Shopping

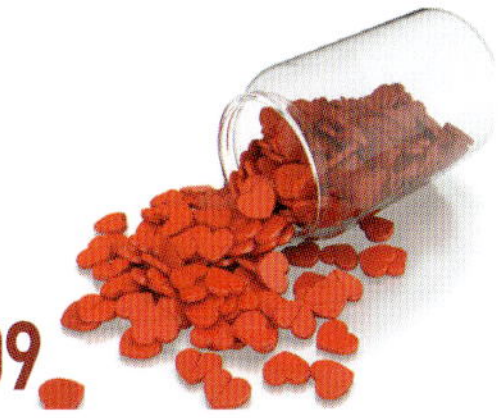

09 Love/ Relationships

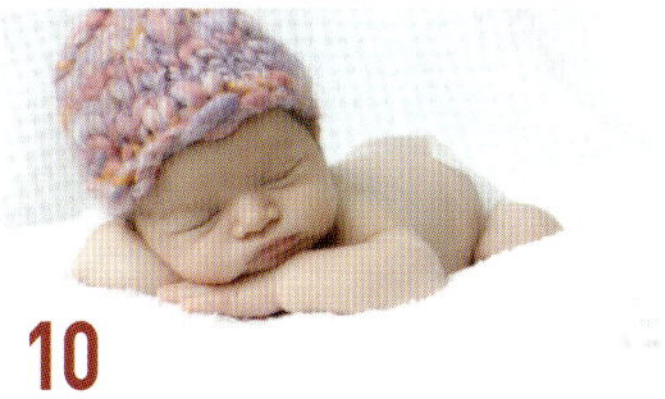

10 Sleeping

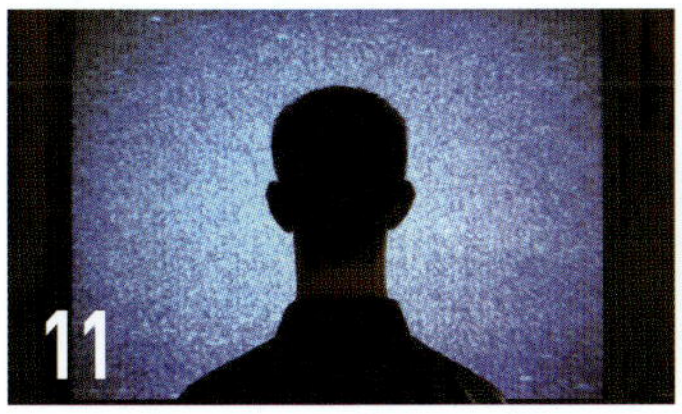

11 Watching television

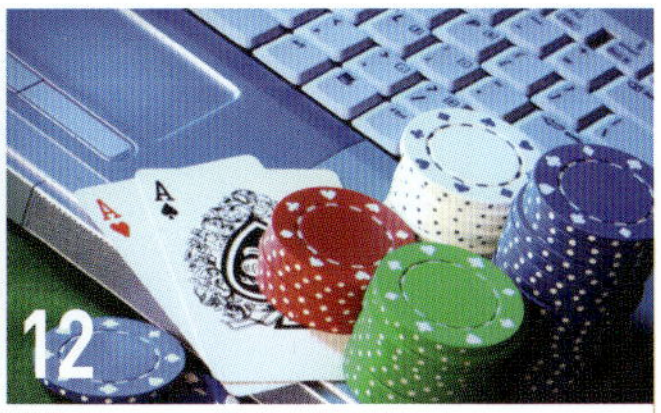

12 Gambling

PART 2 ●

- What is another thing people do to escape reality?
- Do you think this is a good or bad escape? Why?
- Survey your group or class, and make a list of what you all think are the best and worst ways to escape from reality.

grooming *(n.)*: taking care of personal appearance

C. Basements & Lizards™

Create a character and take him or her on a quest unlike anything you have ever seen or heard before!

Part 1 ● Choose a hero from below and give him or her a name. Tell your partner or group your character's name, who you chose, and why.

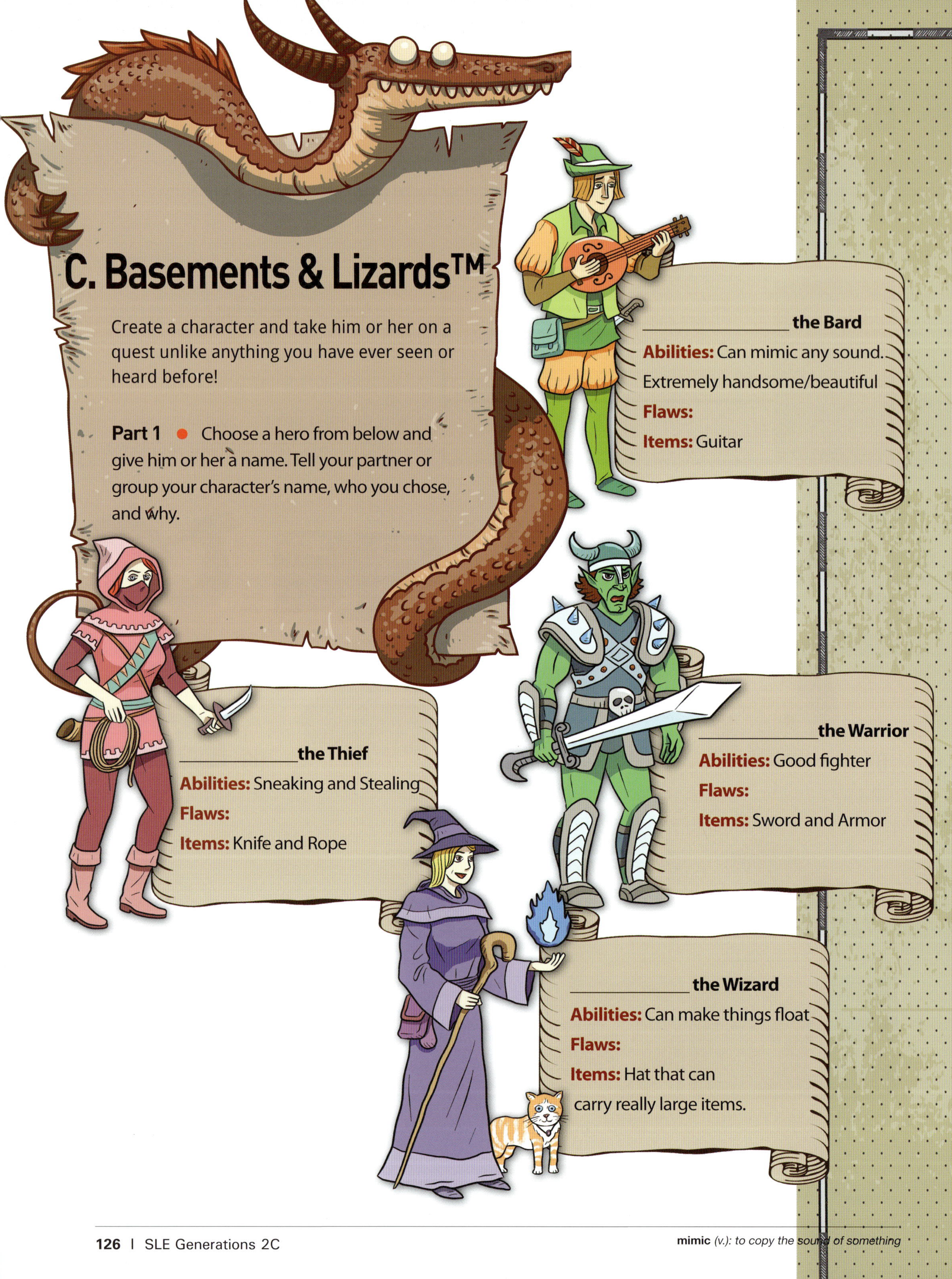

mimic *(v.): to copy the sound of something*

Part 2 ● Choose two extra abilities for your character. Be careful what you choose as each ability comes with a flaw. Tell your partner/group which abilities you chose and why.

Ability: Very brave **Flaw:** Really Shy	**Ability:** Can jump really high **Flaw:** Fear of heights	**Ability:** Super smart **Flaw:** Really boring	**Ability:** Doesn't feel pain **Flaw:** Out of shape
Ability: Enhanced eyesight **Flaw:** Afraid of the dark	**Ability:** Super fast **Flaw:** Extremely lazy	**Ability:** Can hold breath for long time **Flaw:** Can't swim	**Ability:** Born leader **Flaw:** Gets lost easily
Ability: Excellent public speaker **Flaw:** Terrible memory	**Ability:** Gets stronger from beer **Flaw:** Gets angry when drinking	**Ability:** Can speak to animals **Flaw:** Afraid of animals	**Ability:** Can heal injuries **Flaw:** Hypochondriac

Choose an extra item that you think your character could use on the quest.

hypochondriac *(n.)*: someone who is always worried about being sick

Part 3 ● Work with your team to decide how to overcome each situation. Consider your abilities and items, and use your imagination to think up creative solutions to each situation.

- When your team wants to try something, you must flip a coin.
- Heads means you succeed and you can move on to the next space.
- Tails means something went wrong and you must try a different plan before moving.

Example: There is a troll standing in the road!

A: *I'm going to attack the troll with my sword! Tails. Oh no, I must have missed!*

B: *I will take an apple out of my hat and give it to the troll as a gift. Heads. Success! Apparently, the troll likes apples.*

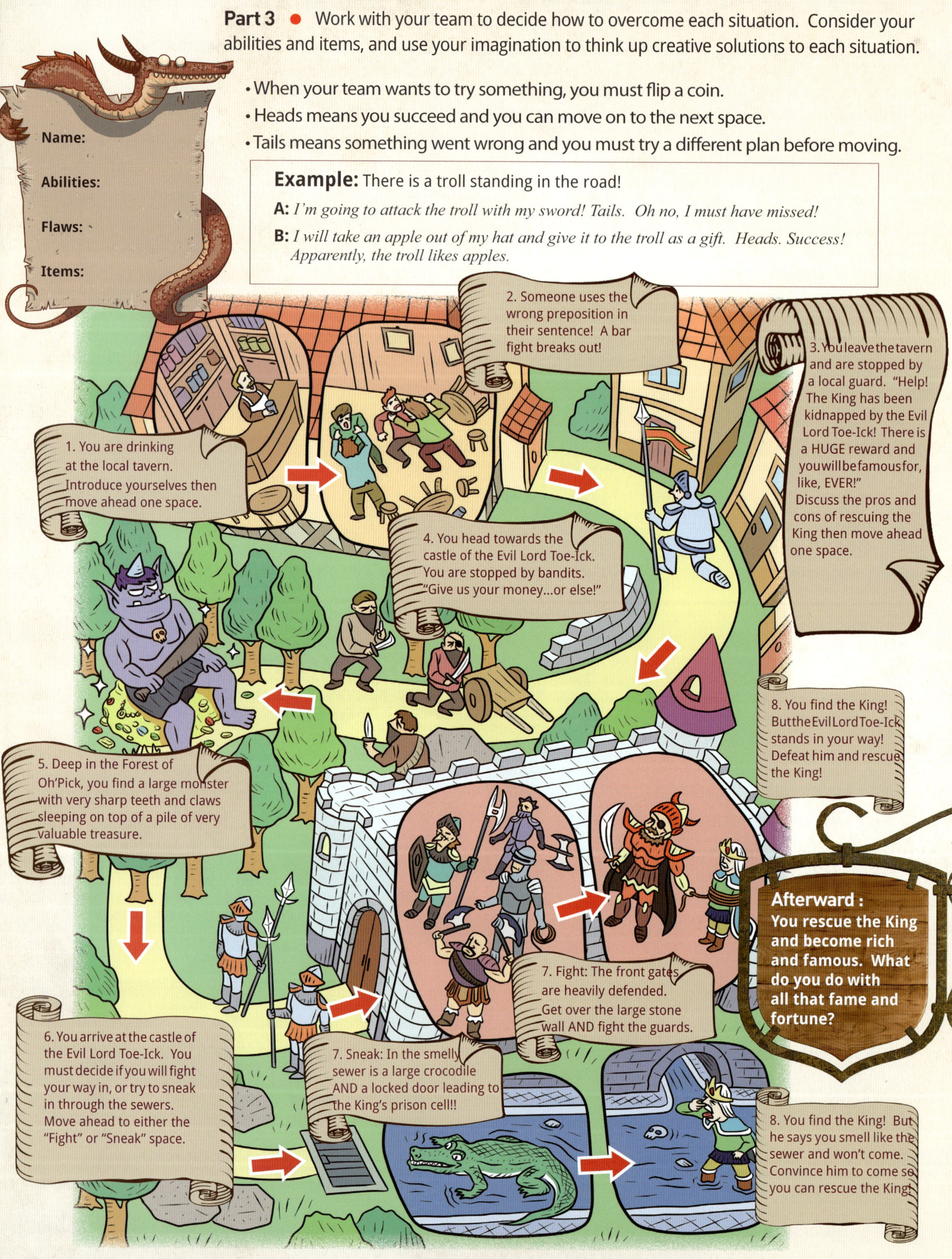

Discussion Questions

1 What do you like to do when you need to escape from life's troubles?

- ▶ What is something you used to do to escape that you no longer do? Why did you stop?

2 Most children have a vivid imagination. Why do we lose this as we grow up and become adults?

- ▶ Do you think modern conveniences, from televisions to video games to smart phones, make it harder to use our imagination and creativity? Why or why not?
- ▶ Do you think that having a good imagination is important for success in life?

3 What's the difference between being optimistic and unrealistic?

- ▶ Do you know anyone who seems to live with their head in the clouds?

4 Have you ever been **hypnotized**?

- ▶ Would you like to be? Why or why not?
- ▶ Have you ever visited a fortune teller?

5 What is something you would like to do but don't think will be possible even **in your wildest dreams**?

- ▶ Is it good to **live out** our fantasies, or better to keep them to ourselves?
- ▶ What do you think about dressing up in costumes or other forms of fantasy or roleplay?

6 What science fiction or fantasy story has **captured your imagination**?

- ▶ What did you like about it?
- ▶ How has the story influenced your life?

7 If you wrote a science fiction or fantasy story,

- ▶ Where would the story take place?
- ▶ How can science fiction influence real science?

UNIT 7 REVIEW

How well can you use:

- ☐ Expressions that show skepticism?
- ☐ The verb "wish"?

What do you need to study more?

hypnotize *(verb):* to put someone into a hypnotic state
capture someone's imagination *(idiom):* to interest someone in a lasting way
live out *(phrasal verb):* to do something previously imagined
in your wildest dreams *(phrasal verb):* ever; in your imagination

Activity :Build-a-Beast

Develop your own monster or mysterious happening.

Example

Appearance	*An adult-sized human covered in marshmallow crème*
Location	*Hides in dark alleys near bakeries*
Actions	*He will attack those eating marshmallow and steal their marshmallow-based food products. Needs them to keep his "skin" fluffy.*
Origins	*Guy was trying to set the World Record for Largest S'More. Something went horribly wrong.*
Name	*The Marshmallow Maniac*

Appearance What does the monster look like?	
Location Where does the monster live?	
Actions What does the monster do? What happened to make people believe it is real?	
Origins How did it all start?	
Name What is it called?	

Lisa InWonderland : So that's my dream…what do you think?

DoorKnobPhobia: Very interesting. The choices you make in your dream suggest you are very scared. First, you are in a scary attic with a mirror. Mirrors are safe things in the real world. But this mirror is scary in your dream! And the area with three doors? Three different fears you must choose from! You chose the door that lead to exams – are you afraid of your education? And your boyfriend, too? At the end of your dream, you hide in your bed. Stop hiding! Face your fears!

BogglestheMind: That's some pretty crazy stuff, girl! You must be more careful about what you eat before you go to bed.

JustACigar19: If the whole dream took place "inside the mirror", I think this is really a dream about how you view yourself. Falling is usually a sign that you feel like you're not in control. Maybe it has something to do with having so many choices in your life right now? Doors often represent choices. Notice you didn't even choose door three for yourself – you followed this Mr. Squiggles fellow through it. It sounds like you should start organizing your schedule better. Start a 'to do' list!

CrazyHairGurl51: You should listen to your dream! Dreams are windows into the future. According to your dream, you will start a family with your boyfriend…but only after you deal with some big exam. Do you have finals coming up? Do you think he might pop the question? Let me be the first to say congratulations!

A. Discussion

1. Which interpretation makes the most sense? Why do you think so?
2. People try to find the hidden meaning in things other than just dreams. What are some of the other ways we try to interpret the lives of ourselves and others?

B. Writing

1. Write a new interpretation to Lisa's dream. You can agree with certain parts of other people's interpretations or explain why you think they are wrong.

08 Good Intentions

Success and Failure

Objectives:

/ Define concepts using gerunds
/ Listen to a story about a high school dance

WARM UP

Which of the following people most fits your idea of success? Why?

1 Allie: 40-year-old musical actress, married but no time for kids

2 Aaron: 30-year-old adventurer, climbed most of the world's highest mountains, single, unemployed and lives in parents' basement

3 Don: 45-year-old advertising executive, workaholic, divorced with two kids, rich

4 Margie: 35-year-old stay-at-home mother of three, happily married for ten years

IDIOMS

- **If all else fails**
  It's a big dream, but *if all else fails.* I can always go back to my old job.

- **Key to success**
  In marketing, understanding the customer is the *key to success.*

PHRASAL VERBS

- **Go under**
  It was terrible when their business *went under.* I felt really bad for the family.

- **Pull something off**
  It's going to be really tough to *pull this off,* but when we do, we'll be rich!

COLLOCATIONS

- **Measure success**
  I wouldn't *measure success* by how many degrees a person has. It's more about experience.

- **Without fail**
  Without fail, every time I go to Paris on vacation, it's raining.

TONGUE TWISTER

Theo Thistle is a successful thistle-sifter.
While sifting a sieve full of un-sifted thistles,
he thrust three thousand thistles through the thick of his thumb.

LESSON 1

A. The Ladder to Success

Language Point : Defining Concepts

Gerund phrases can be used to define abstract terms such as success.

Example:

A: *I think success is **having lots of close friends and family.***

B: *I would say that success is **making lots of money.***

PART 1

Choose 5 of the items below that represent your personal idea of success.

Success is...

- ■ ...being married.
- ■ ...living alone.
- ■ ...being powerful.
- ■ ...being independent.
- ■ ...being healthy.
- ■ ...retiring early.
- ■ ...saving lives..
- ■ ...inventing something new.
- ■ ...making other people happy.
- ■ ...having many friends.
- ■ ...being in love.
- ■ ...traveling wherever you want.
- ■ ...being beautiful/handsome.
- ■ ...speaking more than one language.
- ■ ...having children.
- ■ ...being on television.
- ■ ...starting your own business.
- ■ ...being able to purchase anything you want.
- ■ ...having the freedom to ______________.
- ■ ...studying (subject) at (university).
- ■ ...working for ______________________.
- ■ ...other ____________________________.

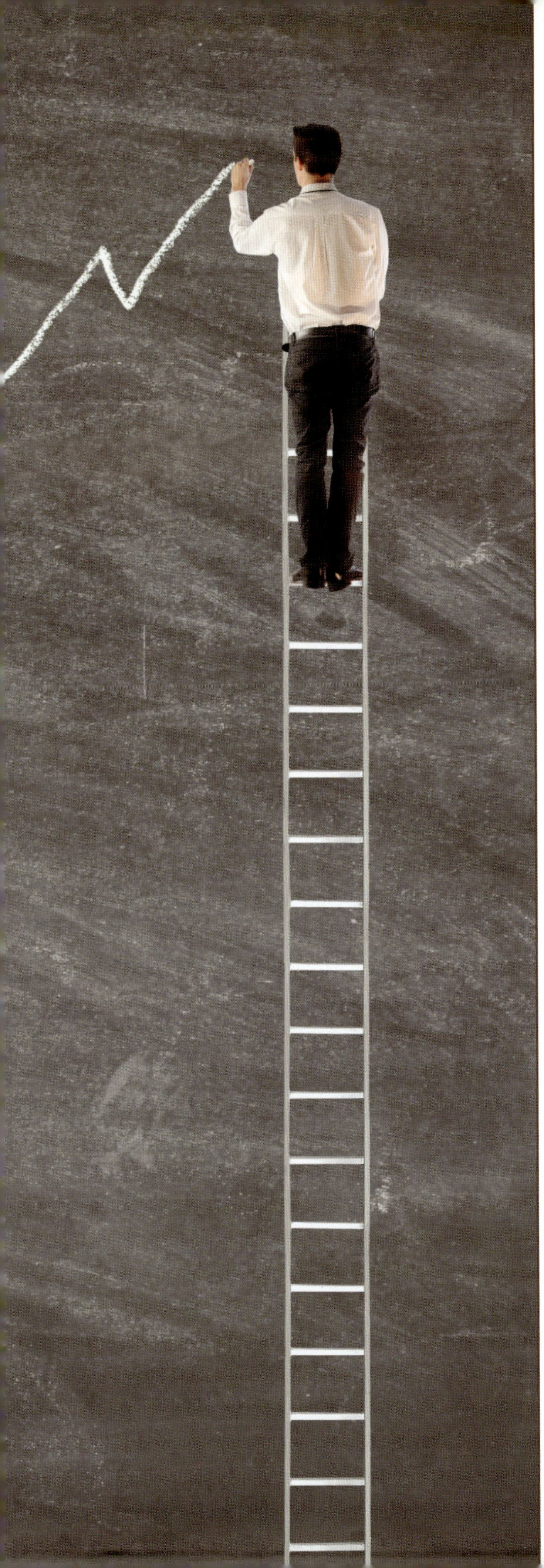

PART 2

Ask your partner or group for their thoughts on what these concepts mean to them.

Example:

What do you think happiness is?

A: *I think that happiness is feeling connected to the people around you.*

B: *I disagree. Happiness is watching your foes fail.*

A: *Wow. You need help.*

B. Cry If I Want To

Pre-listening

How did you celebrate your high school graduation? Based on the picture, pick out all of the things that might be upsetting Susan.

Listening  *TRACK 16-17*

What things did Susan and Richard decide are important? What things don't matter?

What matters...	What doesn't matter...

Post-listening

- What kinds of jobs do Richard and Susan want?
- What does Susan say that life isn't about?
- What does Richard say that life is about?
- Do you agree or disagree with them? Why?

What do you think matters in life? As a class, come up with a list of what matters and doesn't matter

What matters...	What doesn't matter...

C. Growing Pains

• Speculation

Look at the profiles of Richard, Susan, and some of their high school classmates. Speculate on what each classmate might do in the future:

- What do you think their careers might be in the future?
- What interests and hobbies might they have in the future?
- What kind of goals and dreams might they have in the future?
- What might their relationships be like in the future?

Example:

A. I think that Stephanie might become a chef, but she could also become a veterinarian.

Richard:
Favorite class: Composition **Clubs & activities:** Choir, Junior Varsity swim team, Future MBAs Club **Social life:** Captain of the swim team ~ Voted "best writer" by his classmates **Future goal:** To be a doctor

Stephanie:
Favorite class: Biology **Clubs & activities:** Photography Club, Glee Club, Community Service Club **Social life:** Voted "funniest" by her classmates **Future goal:** Knows she wants some sort of job related to animals

Kyle
Favorite class: Discussion & Debate **Clubs & activities:** Varsity football team, Class Treasurer, Jazz Band **Social life:** Voted "most charismatic" by his classmates ~ Voted prom king **Future goal:** To be a professional musician

Susan:
Favorite class: Calculus **Clubs & activities:** Soccer team, Class president, Cooking Club **Social life:** Voted "most likely to succeed" by her classmates **Future goal:** To own her own restaurant

Stan:
Favorite class: Composition **Clubs & activities:** Marching band, Junior Varsity football team, Future MBAs Club **Social life:** Voted "most indecisive" by his classmates **Future goal:** No specific wishes

Paulette:
Favorite class: History **Clubs & activities:** Cooking Club, Swim Team, Chess Club **Social life:** Takes classes at a local college because she says she is bored with high school ~ Voted "most likely to take over the world" by her classmates **Future goal:** To be a lawyer

Relationships:

- Richard, Stan, and Kyle are best friends
- Stephanie, Susan, and Paulette are best friends
- Richard, Stan, Paulette, and Susan have known each other since elementary school
- Richard and Stephanie are dating
- Susan and Kyle are dating

25 years later...

Look at the profiles of Richard, Susan, and some of their high school classmates at their 25-year high school reunion.

- Which information here surprises you? Which information does not surprise you?
- What do you think could have happened to cause each person to reach the point they are at today?
- Which classmate seems the most successful? Which classmate seems the least successful? Explain your choice.

Example:

I'm surprised that Susan married Richard when she was Kyle's girlfriend in high school. I wonder if they are still friends.

Stan:
Interests & Hobbies: Watching television, playing golf **Career Notes:** Vice President of a chain of fast food restaurants **Wishes:** No specific wishes

Stephanie:
Interests & Hobbies: Walking her pet dog with her family, church choir **Career Notes:** Veterinarian **Wishes:** To start her own greeting card company featuring photos of animals, to open her own veterinary clinic

Richard:
Interests & Hobbies: Cooking, reading newspapers **Career Notes:** Assistant Director of Marketing at a small company **Wishes:** To retire from his marketing job and become a freelance journalist

Susan:
Interests & Hobbies: Reading non-fiction books, watching movies **Career Notes:** Owns her own catering company **Wishes:** To open a café featuring her own homemade muffins and cookies

Paulette:
Interests & Hobbies: Swimming, baking **Career Notes:** Lawyer at a well-known law firm **Wishes:** To become a partner at her law firm

Kyle:
Interests & Hobbies: Playing saxophone in a jazz band, coaching his son's football team **Career Notes:** High school Civics teacher **Wishes:** To help his son go to college on a scholarship, to become mayor of his city

Relationships:

- Richard, Stan, and Kyle are still friends
- Susan and Paulette are still friends. They have lost touch with Stephanie.
- Richard and Susan are married

Discussion Questions

1 Does your definition of success match your parents' definition of success?

- In what ways don't your definitions match?

2 Have you ever had a reunion with your high school classmates?

- If so, how did it go?
- If not, would you like to have a reunion?

3 What do you feel has been your biggest accomplishment in your life so far?

4 Do you think that mistakes and failures can lead to later success, or are mistakes always bad?

- What have you learned from your failures?

5 Think of a time when you were successful at something. What was the situation?

- What was the **key to that success**?
- What part does luck play in success?

6 Have you been successful studying English? Why or why not?

7 Can you think of a company that has **gone under**?

- What do you think contributed to the company's failure?

8 How important is it to have a backup plan **if all else fails**? Why?

key to success *(idiom)*: the way to become successful
go under *(phrasal verb)*: to bankrupt a business
if all else fails *(idiom)*: something you will do if your plans do not succeed

LESSON 2

>> WARM UP

Objectives:
/ Discuss life decisions and concepts of success

GOOD INTENTIONS

What do you think the symbols above mean in relation to being successful? Rank the symbols from most important to least important based on what you think is necessary for success.

◇ **Note: The three activities that follow may be done separately or combined into a game. The score from each activity continues into the next with a result at the end.**

A. Build a You

- From the rows below, ask questions to a partner or group to make a character or choose which areas best fit your own life. Be sure to ask why they chose what they did.
- Based on the numbers listed for each option you choose, add up the points from each category and put the total into the box on the right.

$	Time	Family	Fame

GENDER	♂ MALE	♀ FEMALE	Time	$ Money	Family / Fame
EDUCATION *What kind of degree do you want? Why?*	*None* Time +2	**High School** Time +1 $ +1	**Bachelors** $ +2	**Masters** $ +3 Time -1	**Doctorate** $ +3 Time -2 Fame +1
RELATIONSHIP *What are you looking for in a partner? Why?*	*SINGLE* Time +2	**Boyfriend Girlfriend** Time +1 $ -1	**Married** Time -1 $ +1	Family +2	
CHILDREN *How many children do you want? Why?*	*None* Time +2	**Kristin** Time -1 $ -1 Family +1 *Writing, Singing*	**Lee** Time -1 $ -1 Family +1 *Making Things, Fighting Crime*	**Ian** Time -1 $ -1 Family +1 *Sports, Food*	**Stephen & Ruda** Time -1 $ -1 Family +1 *Fashion, Fighting*
JOB *What kind of job do you want? Why?*	*None* Time +2	**Part-time Worker** $ +1 Time -1	**Office Worker** $ +2 Time -2	**Manager** $ +3 Time -3	**Business Owner** $ +4 Time -5 Fame +2

B. Life Choices

For each choice, discuss what you would do in the situation. Give a reason why you would choose yes or no.		$	Clock	Family	Star
	Points from Activity A:				
1. You have a chance to make a large amount of money working in a small, secluded country. The contract is three years. *Will you go?*					
YES $ +3 Family -2	**NO** $ -1 Clock +1 Family +1				
2. You have been contacted by the local orphanage. A new government bill will give additional financial support to adoptive families. *Do you adopt?*					
YES Family +1 $ +1 Clock -2	**NO** *NO CHANGE*				
3. You have the opportunity to run for a political office. *Do you run?*					
YES $ -2 Star +2 *You had to spend a lot, but you are elected!*	**NO** Clock +2				
4. You've been asked to help out in a top secret government mission. You can go only if you have two or fewer Star. *Do you risk it?*					
YES $ +1 Clock -1 *In return they can* ***pull some strings*** *and get you a promotion ONLY if you're an Office Worker.* *(Office Worker* $ *+2)*	**NO** *NO CHANGE*				

5. You have the opportunity to learn a new instrument. *Do you? What instrument? Why?* **YES** $ -1 +1 -1 — **NO** +2				
6. Taking the bus is a pain. *Do you buy a new car?* **YES** $ -2 +1 — **NO** $ +2				
7. You are invited on Single's Cruise. You can go only if you aren't married. *Do you set sail?* **YES** +1 $ -1 *You meet a wonderful person. BONUS: You can get married if you want!* $ +1 +2 — **NO** *NO CHANGE*				
8. A week long training opportunity! You can go only if you have a job. *Do you say yes?* **YES** -1 $ +1 — **NO** +1 +2				
9. You are thinking about changing jobs and becoming a monk. *Is it time for some deep contemplation?* **YES** $ -3 -2 +3 — **NO** -2				
10. You are offered a chance to be on a reality TV show. *Do you want 15 minutes of fame?* **YES** +3 $ +1 -2 -1 — **NO** +1				

C. Good Intentions

As a group, flip a coin to move ahead (heads: one space, tails: two spaces). If you land on...

CHANCE: each person chooses one of the numbers for themselves, then look on the next page.

SITUATION: every person who answers gets the points.

CHOICE: choose your own answer and explain why you made that choice.

START

With your whole life ahead of you...

01 CHOICE

You have figured out a way to cheat on your taxes. Do it?

- **YES** Flip a coin: Heads $ +3
- TAILS: You are caught, spend time in jail! -1 +1
- **NO** $ -1

06 SITUATION

Bad economy. You need to downsize your budget. What is something in your day-to-day life that you will give up to save money? Why?

- $ +1

07 CHOICE

Your car breaks down

- Do you fix it yourself? -2
- Do you pay someone to do it $ -2

08 CHANCE

1  12

09 SITUATION

You want a little more time to relax. What is one thing you can cut out of your schedule to free up time? Why?

- +1

10 CHANCE

3  11

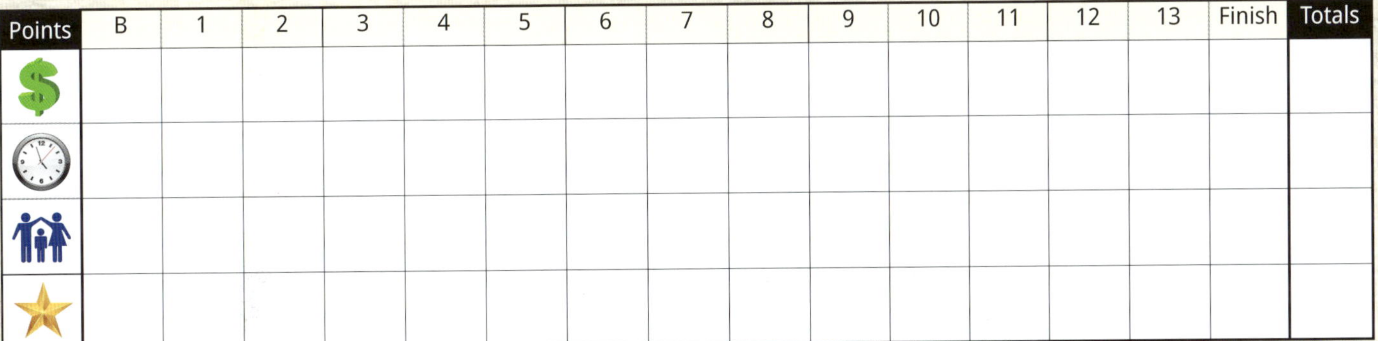

Points	B	1	2	3	4	5	6	7	8	9	10	11	12	13	Finish	Totals
$																
🕒																
👪																
★																

02 SITUATION

Your best friend has a child. Their child's report card was very bad. Give your friend advice.

👪 +1

03 CHOICE

Adopt a pet

YES 👪 +1 $ -1 🕒 -1

NO 🕒 +1

What kind of pet would you adopt?

04 SITUATION

You've started a blog. What is it about? Be specific.

★ +1

05 CHANCE

2 9 10

11 CHOICE

Your parents can no longer take care of themselves.

Do you take them in? 👪 +1 🕒 -1

Or put them in a home? $ -2 🕒 +1

12 CHANCE

5 7 8

13 FINAL DECISION

Do you ditch your career and become an actor, singer, painter, baseball player, etc? What do go for?

YES Flip a coin: Heads ★ +3 $ +2

TAILS: $ -2

NO 🕒 +1 👪 +1

FINISH

Do you want to retire early?

YES $ -3 🕒 +2

NO 🕒 -1 👪 -1 $ +2

CHANCE!

01
You published a book!
What was it about? Now you have to sign lots of autographs.

-1 $ +1 +1

02
Demoted! Lose one level at your job. *What bad habit do you think got you demoted?*

$ -1

03
Embarrassing situation. *What happened that made you so embarrassed?*

-1

04 News interview! You were interviewed on a major news network. *What was the interview about?*

+1

05 Sudden surgery! It's okay, you didn't need that organ anyway. You also get lots of bed rest! *What happened?*

+1 $ -1

06 Uh-oh. Big unpaid debt. *What did you buy on credit?*

$ -1

07 Oopsie, baby! Congrats on the new baby. *What do you name the little bundle of joy?*

-1 $ -1 +1

08 You won a national beauty contest! You're in high demand! *What shows are you going to appear on?*

+2 -1

09 Promoted!
$ +1 What's your new title?
If you are a "business owner":
$ +2 for opening a new store.
What kind of business is it?

10 Employee of the Month!
What good habit do you think got you the award?

+1  +1

11 Holy cow, you won the lotto!
What do you plan to do with the money?

$ +3

12 Someone robbed a bank, and they look just like you!
Did you do it?

+1

Score Card

	Negative Points	1-4	5-10	11-15
$	How's life under the bridge?	You managed to scrape by but you couldn't afford a lot of luxuries.	You lived comfortably. You had what you needed and much of what you wanted.	You have more money than you know what to do with!
	You're so busy, it's unhealthy! Hope you have time to see a doctor!	You barely found time for yourself. You daydream of a vacation...	Your time management skills are excellent!	You're as free as a bird! You are the envy of your busy friends!
	You don't even recognize yourself in the mirror.	You get a friendly nod from people in your neighborhood.	You sometimes notice people staring at you in public.	What's it like to be so famous? Can I have your autograph?
	...All by yourself, Apparently you wanna be, all by yourself...	You sometimes wish you had a little more support when times are tough.	You are surrounded by a loving and supportive family.	You might as well be the Mafia you have so much family.

Discussion **Questions**

1 Based on this lesson, what do you seem to value most in life: time, money, fame, or family?

- ▶ Based on your results, would you like to change any of your values?

2. Who in your life do you view as a role model for successful living? Why?

3. How do you measure success?

- ▶ What does success taste like?
- ▶ Is success a journey or a destination?

4. What responsibilities does the government have in helping citizens to be more successful?

- ▶ Do you think it's possible to teach someone to become successful?
- ▶ Do you believe that people must work hard to become successful?

5. Who do you think is the most successful person in your country?

- ▶ What part does luck play in success?
- ▶ Does success make a person happy?

6. What is something you have tried to pull off, but didn't succeed?

- ▶ Can you think of an example of a famous failure?
- ▶ Do you think most people fail before they succeed?

7. What can you do now to be more successful in the future?

How well can you use:

☐ Gerunds to define concepts?

What do you need to study more?

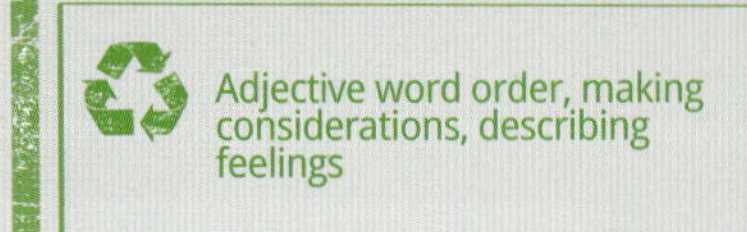

Activity : Dress for Success

Advise the people below on what to wear to succeed in each situation.

- What needs to be considered?
- Describe at least 5 things that each of the people below should wear.

Example: I'm going on a 20-km hike today, and it's supposed to rain the whole time! What should I wear?

You should consider what the terrain is like. You should also consider what the temperature is. If it's not too cold, wear shorts so that the legs of your pants won't get muddy...

Part 1

I didn't have time to shop for a costume, and I'm going to a costume party. I want my friends to be shocked by my costume. What can I put together quickly?

I am going on a date tonight at a fancy restaurant. I want to dress nicely, but I also want my date to be amazed by my unique style. What should I wear?

My friend is having a New Year's party. The invitation says to dress formally. I want my friend to be content with my outfit. What should I wear?

My friend is having a wedding at a beach that is famous for its hot weather. What could I wear that would look dressy but also allow me to enjoy walking on the beach?

I'm going to play tennis with the CEO of my company today. I want to look put-together, but not overdressed. What would be something that's appropriate for a tennis game?

I am worried about my interview for a job with a luxury brand company. I can't afford their clothing, but I want to make a good impression! What should I wear?

I am going to a work event and the dress code is "smart casual". My boss will be angry at me if I look too casual, though. What should I wear?

Part 2

1. Have you ever worried about what to wear? Why were you worried? What did you decide to wear in the end?
2. Have you ever been horrified or amazed by an outfit? Why did you feel that way? Describe the outfit.
3. Can being fashionable make a person more or less successful?

Segue

The South Forsyth High School Reunion Society

Presents

Where Are They Now?

Stan Neville

An understated success story, Stan is the Vice President of the popular fast food chain, "McWendy King". His colleagues say that he is "exceptionally open-minded, and never tells a customer no!"

Married with seven children.

Paulette Martinez

Paulette made a name for herself by graduating top of her class from the prestigious law school of 'Cheatum U". She is currently an associate attorney at the firm of 'Bickers & Bickers'.

Unmarried.

Richard Thompson

Richard is climbing the corporate ladder. He is an assistant director of marketing at a mid-sized firm, where he has started a company-wide newspaper, "Know News, Good News". He and his wife, Susan, recently welcomed a new baby, Jane, into the world.
Married with three children.

Susan (Carr) Thompson

What's that smell? It's the delicious smell of culinary success! Susan owns her own catering company (which has graciously agreed to cater this year's reunion) and has prepared meals for celebrities and politicians!
Married with three children.

Kyle Bartowski

Kyle is a high school history teacher. He coaches little league football for his son, Chase. He also plays in a jazz band, "The Bill the Robot Quintet". He invites you all to come down and hear them play!

Married with one child.

Stephanie Lee-Rickman

Stephanie has taken her love of animals to heart. A veterinarian for over ten years, Stephanie has recently started her own line of trendy greeting cards featuring cute, injured animals.

Married with no children.

Want to find out more about them and everybody else? Well, come on down to the SFHS Thirty Year Reunion! It'll be something to remember... at least until the next reunion!

A. Discussion

1. Which of the people above do you think is the most successful? Why?
2. Do you keep in touch with your friends from high school? Are you ever surprised by how much they've changed? Have any stayed the same?

B. Writing

Imagine that you will be attending a high school reunion soon. Consider what kinds of things you would want your former classmates to know about your life and accomplishments, then write a bio of yourself!

09 Make It Up As You Go

Storytelling and Inferences

Objectives:

/ Make inferences to fill in missing information
/ Listen to a story about a hike

WARM UP

A protagonist is the man character of a story. Brainstorm three famous protagonists:

1. ______________________________
2. ______________________________
3. ______________________________

An antagonist is someone who opposes the protagonist. Brainstorm three famous antagonists:

1. ______________________________
2. ______________________________
3. ______________________________

Who are the protagonists and antagonists in your favorite story?

IDIOMS

- **The story of my life**
  Every time I meet a nice guy, it turns out he has a girlfriend. It's *the story of my life*.
- **Truth is stranger than fiction**
  I didn't exaggerate the details at all. Sometimes *truth is stranger than fiction*.

PHRASAL VERBS

- **Make up**
  Did that really happen, or are you just *making it up*?
- **Plot out**
  We should sit down and *plot out* the details of the trip.

COLLOCATIONS

- **Take place**
  The movie *takes place* in a not so distant future where everyone speaks the same language.
- **Make a long story short**
  To *make a long story short* I forgot your present on the bus.

TONGUE TWISTER

Tell the tall tale of a tall tailed dog
That Tim told to tap a tall ale.

LESSON 1

A. Fables and Foibles

PART 1

- Using the pictures below as a guide, tell the story with your partner. Include a description of the plot and what the characters say in each panel.

> **Example:**
> *In the grasshopper and the ant, there's a lazy grasshopper that doesn't do any work. In A, the grasshopper asked the ants why they're spending all day working. The ant said...*

- Discuss the **moral** of each story. How does the story teach the lessons listed? What other lessons does it teach?

> **Example:**
> *I think that the moral of this story is that everyone should....*

- Try to relate it to a personal story of your own or a situation where it could be applicable.

> **Example:**
> *This reminds me of a time when...*

1. The Grasshopper and the Ant

associate *(verb)*: mix socially
fable *(n.)*: story that teaches a lesson
persistence *(n.)*: the action of doing something without quitting
reap what you sow *(idiom/proverb)*: everything that happens to you is a result of your own actions
subordinates *(n.)*: those of lesser rank

2. The Tortoise and the Hare

Possible lessons

patience, **persistence**, pride leading to **arrogance**

3. The Boy Who Cried Wolf

Possible lessons

trust, lying, responsibility

4. The Lion and the Mouse

Possible lessons

pride, size doesn't matter, be nice to your **subordinates**

5. The Scorpion and the Frog

Possible lessons

human nature, the people you **associate** with, being **gullible**, learning to swim

PART 2 ● Now take one of the stories and retell it as a modern tale.

Example: *The Boy Who Cried Wolf* → *The Boy Who Texted Wolf*

NFERENCE IS A GUESS ABOUT WHAT HAPPENED IN A ST
SAYING OR ON YOUR KNOWLEDGE OF THE SUBJECT. AN

B. Reading Between the Lines

Language Point : Filling in Missing Information with Inferences

An inference is a guess about what happened in a story from clues. These clues can be based on what the characters are saying or on your knowledge of the subject.

A: *He was so hot and thirsty. There was nothing but sand as far as he could see.*
B: *He must have been in the desert because it was so hot and there was a lot of sand and no water.*

Pre-listening

The pictures below tell two different stories. Decide whether the pictures belong to story A or story B depending on what you see. Make a guess as to where the story took place, who was there, and what happened.

Listening  TRACK 18-19

Jack and Lisa are remembering a story of a trip they took when they were younger. Which story are they recounting? Listen for the details that happen between the pictures.

Yosemite National Park Story A

Saguaro National Monument Story B

Javelina *(n.)*: a wild pig-like animal, also known as a peccary

NFERENCE IS A GUESS ABOUT WHAT HAPPENED IN A ST

SAYING OR ON YOUR KNOWLEDGE OF THE SUBJECT. AN

RENCE IS A GUESS ABOUT WHAT HAPPENED IN A STORY

Post-listening

Make up a story based on each series of pictures below. Where there is a blank box, fill in what you think happened.

Step 1 Choose a time and location where the story takes place, and give the character a name.

Example: *Last Thursday, Brenda went to the bank.*

#. 01

#. 02

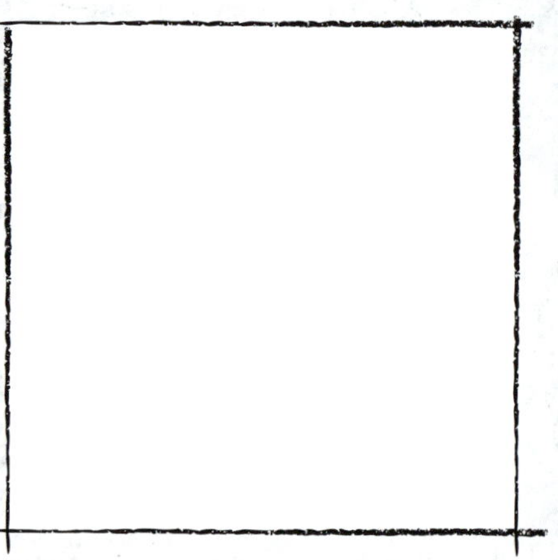

#. 03

Step 2 Tell the story, giving as much detail as possible for each box. Ask information question to move the story along.

Example: *Why did Brenda go to the bank? She went because she needed to take out a loan for a new house. What happened when she went inside?*

#. 04

#. 05

C. The Black Out

• Past speculation

You had a brilliant night. You think. You don't really remember. Look at the items below to piece together a story about what happened last night.

Example:

A: *Well, we might have gone to the beach.*
B: *I'm guessing because…*

A pair of broken sunglasses

A matchbook from the "Dance & Dine" Club downtown

A receipt for twelve copies of the same cookbook

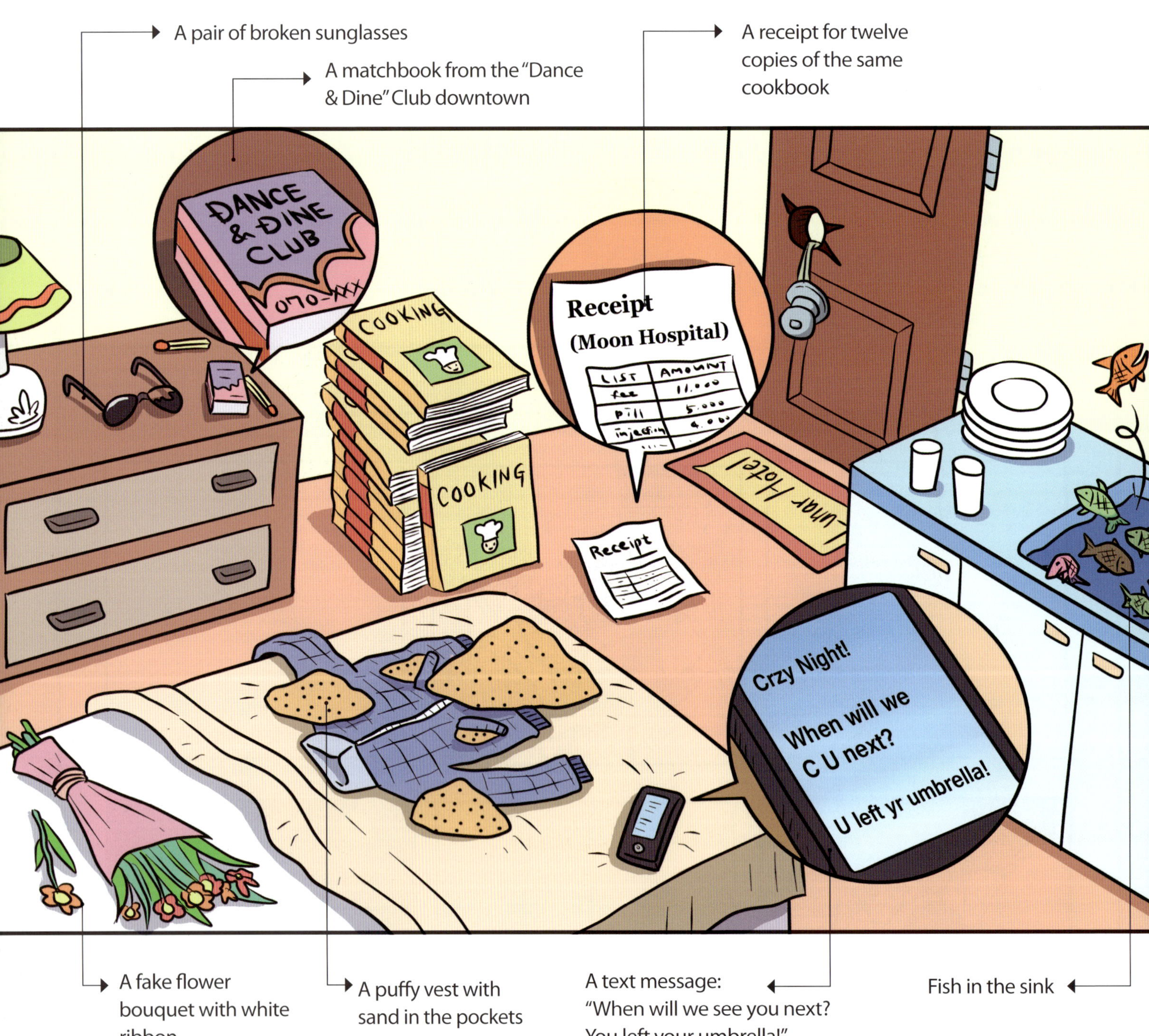

A fake flower bouquet with white ribbon

A puffy vest with sand in the pockets

A text message: "When will we see you next? You left your umbrella!"

Fish in the sink

Discussion **Questions**

1 What is the best method for telling a story? (Book, Movie, Game, Song, etc.)

- ▶ Why do you think so?
- ▶ In what setting do you like stories to take place?

2 What are some important lessons taught in the fables you heard as a child?

- ▶ Do you think these lessons are still relevant in today's world?
- ▶ Who told you stories when you were a child? What kind of stories did they tell you?

3 Do you think stories that are **made up** are more interesting, or do you prefer to hear true stories?

- ▶ Can you give an example of the truth being stranger than fiction?

4 What kind of stories do you like to read?

- ▶ What makes a story really interesting for you?
- ▶ What makes a story really boring?

5 Who is your favorite literary figure (character)?

- ▶ Why do you like this character?
- ▶ If you could be a character in a well-known story, which story would it be?

6 Other than the protagonist and antagonist, what are some of the other types of characters in stories?

7 Should every story have a happy ending? Why or why not?

- ▶ How do you like stories to end?
- ▶ What's the best ending to a story you can remember?

Once upon a time..

make up *(v.)*: to create

LESSON 2

>> WARM UP

Objectives:
/ Describe and develop characters
/ Practice telling stories

Give a short synopsis of a story or movie you like using the five plot points below.

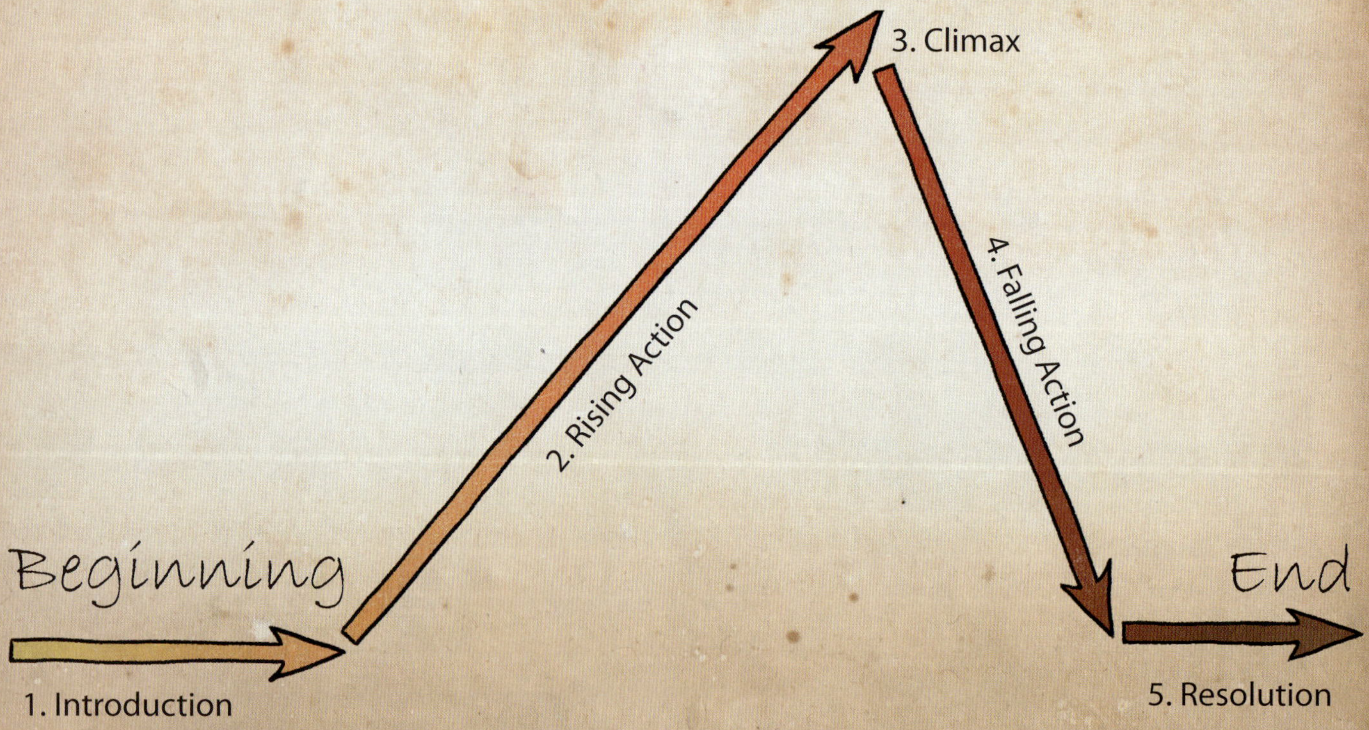

A. Anecdotal Evidence

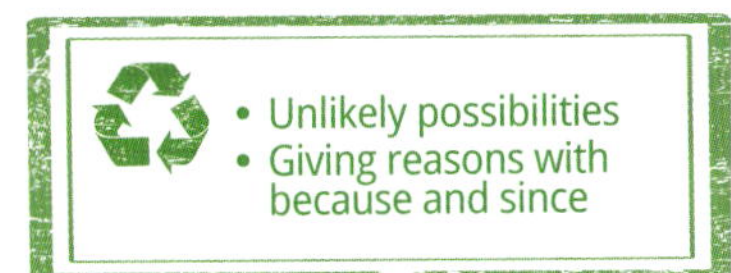

PART 1

Choose a topic below that you would like to interview a classmate about. Think of five interview questions about the topic. As your classmate tells you about the topic, ask follow-up questions to learn as many details as possible about his or her personality.

Example

A: *Tell me about a bad date you've had.*
B: *My first date was a really awkward experience!*

A: *Oh no! Who did you go on the date with?*

B: *I went on the date with Joe, a guy from my high school...*

Topics:

- A time when you helped someone
- An embarrassing moment
- A very happy or proud moment
- A very bad date
- A very sad moment
- A moment that changed your life

PART 2

Now that you've interviewed your classmate and learned a bit more about his or her personality, guess what your classmate might do, or how your classmate might feel, in each of the situations below. Explain the reasons for your guess. After sharing your guesses, discuss whether or not the guesses were correct.

Example

If my partner Joe was invited to be on a reality TV show, I think that he would be the funniest person on the show because...

Your partner...

...has been invited to be on a reality TV show.
In this situation, your partner would...
Your partner definitely would not...

... just found a stray dog on the street.
In this situation, your partner would...
Your partner definitely would not...

...has a 12-hour layover at the airport.
In this situation, your partner would...
Your partner definitely would not...

...was just pickpocketed on the subway.
In this situation, your partner would...
Your partner definitely would not...

B. Get Your Story Straight

Use the following pictures to create a story. You can use the pictures in any order you want. Make sure to use the appropriate verb forms.

C. A Storied Past

Work with a partner or in a group to create a chain story about two people. Use the past tense in the story.

Step 1 Write a profile for two characters.

A	B
A Name: ______________	**B Name:** ______________
Age: ________	**Age:** ________
Sex: ________ **Occupation:** ________	**Sex:** ________ **Occupation:** ________
Interests/Hobbies: ______________	**Interests/Hobbies:** ______________
Adjectives Describing Personality: ________	**Adjectives Describing Personality:** ________

Step 2 Choose the relationship of the characters from above.

Siblings	Lovers	Enemies	Old friends	Complete Strangers

Step 3 Choose a location.

In a train station	Near a famous landmark	On top of a mountain	Around the corner from:	On the other side of:

Chain story *(n.)*: a story written collectively by a group of authors

Step 4 Using the characters and setting chosen from the previous page, make a chain story. Choose a verb and begin the story. After using that verb, cross it off the list. Keep the story going by choosing another verb.

FOUR IN A LINE

Player 1 ● ● **Player 2**

Row 6	Check	Lend	Own	Roll	Stand	Lose	Hope
Row 5	Write	Listen	Cook	Find	Come	Read	Smile
Row 4	Feel	Dream	Clean	Push	Give	Wear	Dance
Row 3	Laugh	Break	Meet	Speak	Take	Swim	Drink
Row 2	Study	Work	Travel	Play	Sing	Walk	Visit
Row 1	Cry	Run	Go	Hit	See	Eat	Sit

Alternate rule : **Link Four Verbs.** Begin with row 1 and choose a verb to start the story. This verb cannot be used again. As the opposing player, you may only choose a verb on the bottom row (row 1), or the verb on row 2 directly above the verb that has been used. Connect four verbs in a row to win!

Discussion Questions

1 Why do you think story telling is an important part of our lives?

- Is it better to **plot out** a story before you tell it, or just make it up as you go?
- How much do people exaggerate when telling personal stories?

2 What are the qualities of a good story?

- What is the most important part of the story - the details or the conclusion?
- Is it better to **make a long story short** or be as detailed as possible?

3 What was the last thing that happened to you that's story-worthy?

4 Can you give a good **anecdote** of a time when you were…

- …late?
- …lost?
- …really hungry or full?
- …scared?
- …heartbroken?

5 What is lost when telling a story through technology? (messenger, email, etc.)

- What is the difference between having someone telling you a story and reading it?

6 What seems to happen to you all the time? In other words, what is the **story of your life**?

7 If your life were a story, what would the title be?

- Who would play you in the movie?
- How would you define the genre?

UNIT 9 REVIEW

How well can you use:

- ☐ Inferences to fill in missing information?
- ☐ English to tell a story

What do you need to study more?

make a long story short *(collocation)*: to sum up a longer series of events
plot out *(phrasal verb)*: to make a detailed plan
anecdote *(n.)*: a short story about a specific moment or event
story of your life *(idiom)*: an expression for when something happens to you that has happened many times before

Activity : The Animal & the Animal

Develop Your Own Fable.

Step 1 Choose a lesson you want to teach. Ask questions about what problems exist in these topics.

Topic areas for lessons:

Health	Safety	Trust/Truth/Lying
Courage	Charity	Planning
Relationships	Work	Education

Step 2 Choose two animals that represent character types. Which adjectives describe the animals' personality?

Rat	Cow	Tiger	Rabbit
Dragon	Snake	Horse	Goat
Monkey	Chicken	Dog	Pig

Step 3 Make up a story with a conflict that teaches your lesson with the animals you chose.

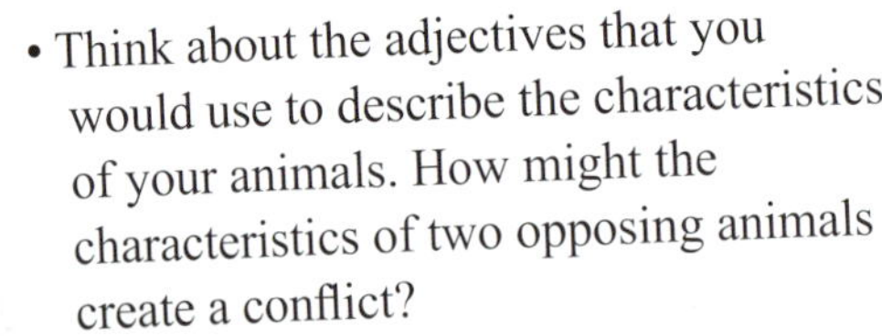

TIPS

- Think about the adjectives that you would use to describe the characteristics of your animals. How might the characteristics of two opposing animals create a conflict?
- In a typical fable one animal usually teaches the other animal a lesson that they don't see at the beginning.

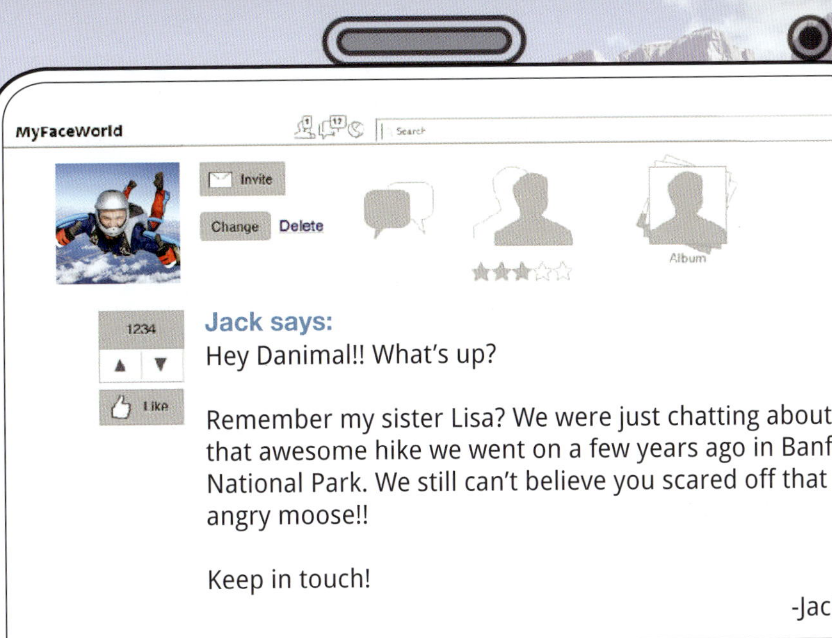

Jack says:
Hey Danimal!! What's up?

Remember my sister Lisa? We were just chatting about that awesome hike we went on a few years ago in Banff National Park. We still can't believe you scared off that angry moose!!

Keep in touch!

-Jack

Dan says:
Jack! What's up, dude?

Life has been good since that hike. I actually just got back from a trip in the Altai mountain range on the borders of Kazakhstan, China, Mongolia, and Russia. I ate some good food, met some amazing people, and saw lots of spectacular views (attaching a photo of one). I didn't even have to scare off any angry animals this time!

Got any hiking plans coming up?

-Dan

Jack says:
No hiking plans yet. I've been doing some work with an awesome band, The Crimson Kings. That's been keeping me pretty busy.

I checked out the photos you took on your trip. Looks like it was awesome!

-Jack

P.S. *You should buddy Lisa, too! She wants to see the photos from your trip.*

Dan says:
Will do! Glad you liked the pics. Keep in touch!

A. Discussion

1. Based on Dan's message and the photo that he sent, what are some inferences that you can make about his trip to Kazakhstan?
2. How often do you keep in touch with old friends and acquaintances via social networking sites? What are some other ways to keep in touch?

B. Writing

Find a photo from a trip you went on or event from your daily life. Write a caption describing the story behind the photo: where it was taken, why it was taken, who you were with, when you took the picture, etc.

10 Looking Back

Bringing It All Together

Objectives:

/ Review language points from previous chapters
/ Evaluate our progress
/ Work on communication and decision making skills

WARM UP

LANGUAGE POINTS SELF EVALUATION:

Look at the following list of topics and skills covered throughout the book. Which topics and skills do you feel comfortable using? Which ones could you review?

Unit 1 Arts and Media

- ☐ Using abstract adjectives
- ☐ Changing the strength of opinions. **Important to / Important for**

Unit 2 Planning and Compromise

- ☐ **-ever** words, raising considerations with **indirect questions**
- ☐ Language for negotiating and compromising

Unit 3 Responsibilities

- ☐ Modals of expectation
- ☐ Discussing responsibility

Unit 4 Dilemmas

- ☐ Stipulating conditions using *even if, only if, and unless*
- ☐ Weighing options

Unit 5 Shopping and Preferences

- ☐ Adjective order
- ☐ **Adjective + preposition** combinations for describing feelings.

Unit 6 Communication Skills

- ☐ Showing interest and word stress
- ☐ Strength of words and exaggeration

Unit 7 Dreams and Escapes

- ☐ Expressing skepticism and belief
- ☐ Using the verb *wish* in the past, present, and future

Unit 8 Success and Failure

- ☐ Defining concepts
- ☐ Discussing what makes success

Unit 9 Storytelling and Inferences

- ☐ Inferring details
- ☐ Telling anecdotes

Evaluation

3 = confident using this skill and will use it in the future.

2 = need practice but have an overall understanding of the skill.

1 = need to work on skill further to feel confident.

42-54 points: Ready for the next level, 3A

30-42 points: Could move on to 3A, but might consider more study in 2C to become accurate.

18-30 points: Need further study in 3A to master skills.

LESSON 1

A. The Devil's Debate

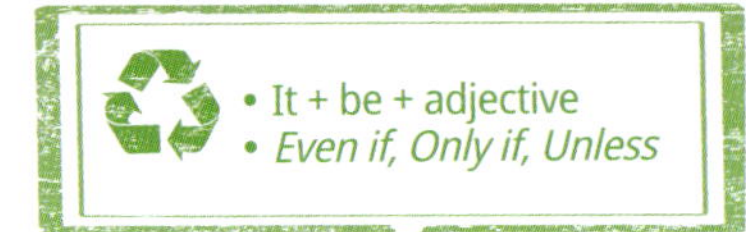

Choose one of the opinions below, and simply say whether you agree or disagree. Your partner(s) MUST disagree with you.

Example: It is acceptable for both men and women to stay at home and take care of children.

A: *I believe that it is perfectly acceptable for men to stay at home.*

B: *I disagree. Even if a man is good with children, it is really important that a mother be with her child when he or she is young.*

1. It is equally acceptable for men and women to stay home and take care of children.

2. English skills are more important than being able to speak your native language well.

3. It is terrible that people have plastic surgery for purely cosmetic reasons.

4. It is good to send children to study abroad during middle and high school.

5. This country would be better run by a woman than a man.

6. It is important that people give up their cars and use public transportion in order to help the environment.

7. It is improper to use cell phones in public places.

8. It is necessary that the government raises income tax by 20% in order to provide completely free education for everyone.

9. Money is the key to happiness.

10. It is important to follow what an elder says even if you disagree.

B. This is the End, Beautiful Friend, the End

Pre-listening

Figure out who is going where and how they are getting there.

Listening

TRACK 20-21

Check your answers to the chart above while listening to the Family's plans for the future.

Post-listening : Bucket List

Looking at the list below, what are some of the things you wish to accomplish in your life?

- Which of these have you already accomplished?
- Which of these do you think you could easily accomplish if you put your mind to it?
- Which ones do you wish you could accomplish, but feel they're impossible? What are some ways of making them possible?

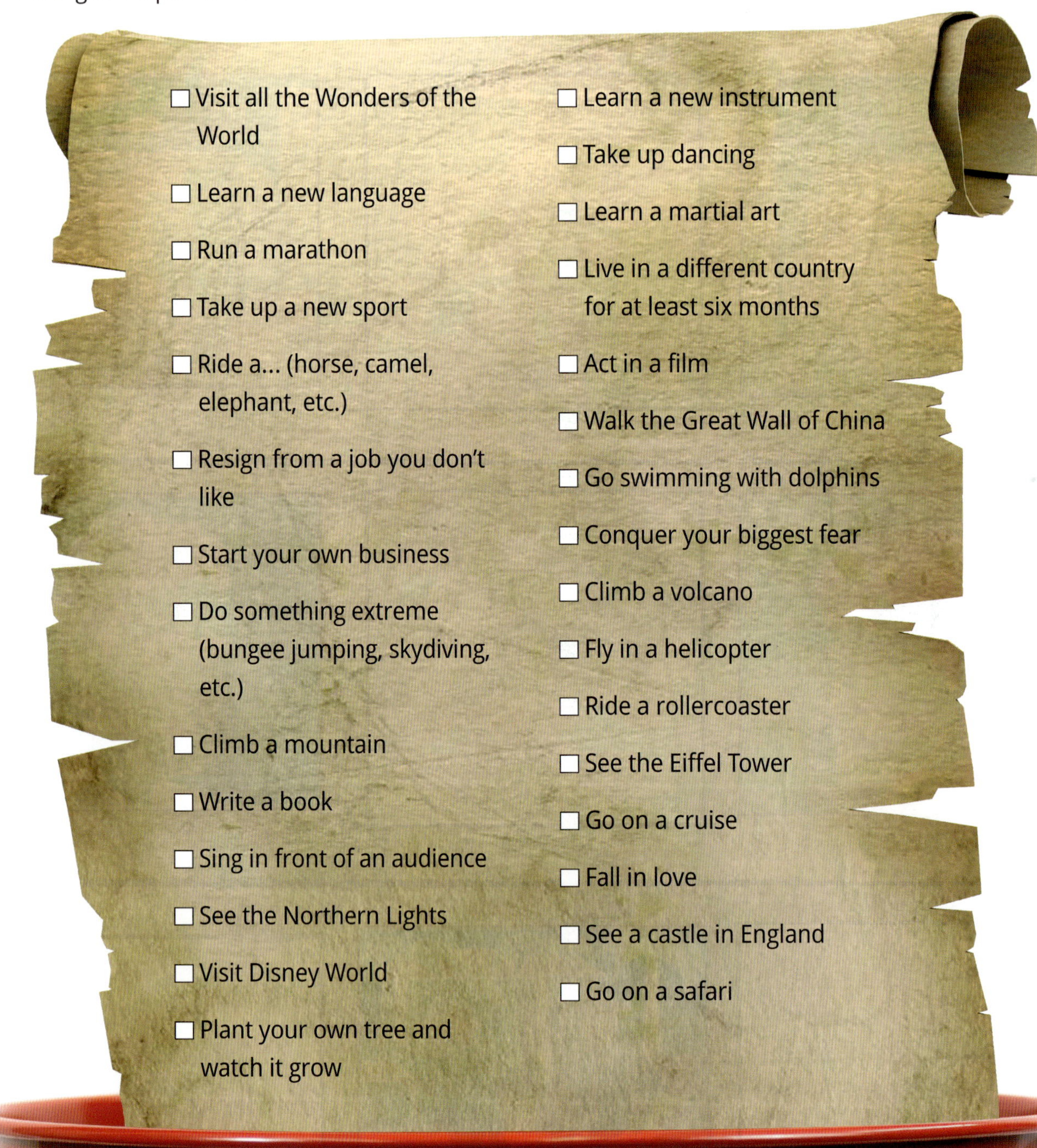

C. The Device

- Planning
- Marketing
- Exaggerating
- Cause and effect
- Comparatives
- Reported speech

You have been given the special task of marketing…the Device! This mysterious box is perfectly square, weighing exactly two kilograms. Decide how exactly the Device should be used, and market it better than the other groups. Lie, exaggerate, and be as creative as possible in selling the Device to the world!

Step 1

Choose a general category for the function of the Device.

Step 2

Brainstorm how the Device solves a problem (or problems) in that category.

Step 3

Plan your marketing campaign for the Device.

Step 4

Present the Device. Explain why your version of the Device is superior to other versions. If another group sounds like they have a better Device, **one up** them!

Categories:

Health	Safety	Energy	Entertainment
Education	Food	Social interaction	Other

Example uses: Does it cure something? Does it make something? Does it prevent something? Does it have an active or a passive use?

The Device	
Function(s)	
Audience	
Price	
Advertising method	
Additional (Slogan, Jingle, etc.)	

D. Comedy of Errors

Divide into teams. One team should flip a coin to move a square (heads: one space, tails: two spaces). After landing on a space, change the incorrect sentence into a correct sentence or follow the **direction**. A correct answer is worth 1 point. The next team flips the coin to move forward. The team with the most points at the end of the game wins!

START	It is important when a painter know perspective.	I put on the bus near my home.	Music is an important genre.	I started working for this company for two years.	My grandfather was died.
I can't ride a horse. -Me too.	I should have drunken last night.	Are you tired? -No I'm tired.	I want whoever can come to the party.	I have my teeth check by a dentist.	You should consider time it will take.
Would you will to see a movie?	He's best singer in the class.	I suppose to meet my friend at six.	This shirt was made by India.	You was sup-pose to meet me here at six!	I have many free times.
You work at home, don't you? -Yes, I don't.	I bought a wool pretty baggy sweater.	Would you rather to go shopping or skating?	I want to new smartphone for my life.	**Say this number:** 604,006,011	What would you do when it is snowing?
I am worried at my future.	I am confusing about that.	I think you might have a big ugly spot on your shirt.	I would call if I have a phone.	My cat died last night. -That's very interesting.	I don't never go the library.
I have been waited in line for three hours!	I'm thirsty. I should have drunken some water.	I sometimes arrive lately.	When you visit my country, you don't keep your shoes on in the house.	I don't never go to the library.	Do you want a large latte? No, I want a large mocha.
I'll cook dinner while I come home.	I will be sleep when you are come home.	**Say this number:** 4,567,890.123	Mails are the worst way to send informa-tion.	I wish that I speak English fluently.	Could you tell me when does finish class.
FINISH	I won't go only if you can come.	There are two monsters on the room.	Do you know she is smart?	The world might been hotter ten years in the future.	He might gone swimming. That's why he's wet.

one-up ***(phrasal v.)*****:** to gain advantage over somebody

E. Review Discussion

Discuss what has happened to the Thompson family so far and talk about yourselves.
Give reasons for your answers and ask follow up questions.

1 What did Grandma Martha think about Lisa's painting?

▶ How would you describe your favorite work of art?

2 How important is it to appreciate fine art?

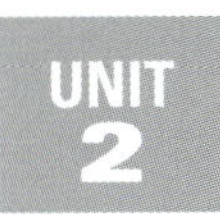

3 What does Richard's friend Stan want to do when they get together?

▶ What is something you like to do whenever you have free time?

4 What are you usually willing to do when making a plan?

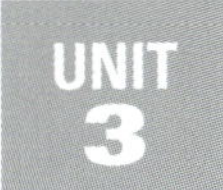

5 What makes Richard a responsible employee?

▶ What responsibilities do you have that you don't like?

6 What is something citizens of your country are supposed to do?

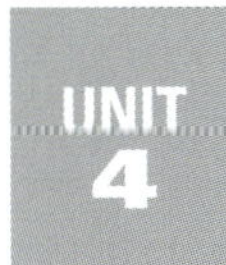

7 What dilemma does Lisa have regarding her friend?

▶ What would you do if you saw your friend at a movie with someone who wasn't their boyfriend/girlfriend?

8 What is something you think you need to live? What is something you want but don't need?

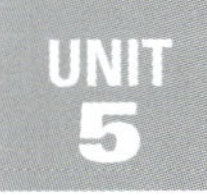

9 How long has it been since Grandpa Charles bought a new cell phone?

▶ What adjectives would you use to describe your cell phone?

10 What product or company are you completely satisfied with?

11 What are Susan and Richard having a conversation about?

▶ How does the meaning change when stressing different words in this sentence: There are several pieces of cake in the fridge.

12 How would you exaggerate this sentence: I went to an exciting party last night.

13 What happened to Lisa in her dream?

▶ What do you think it means if you lose your teeth in a dream?

14 What is something you wish had happened to you in the past, but it did not happen?

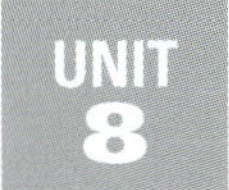

15 Did Susan think she was successful in high school?

▶ How would you define the concept of success?

16 What is the most important component of being successful?

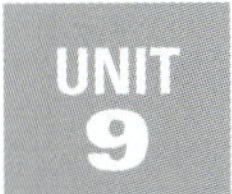

17 What happened on Lisa and Jack's trip?

▶ Do you prefer stories that are told with a lot of detail, or stories that you have to figure out?

18 How would your life be different if you had been born in the U.S. or Canada?

19 Which family member is doing what in the future?

▶ What are your plans for the immediate future?

20 Are you studying English next month?

Activity :Haiku

A haiku is a poem with a very specific structure based on the number of syllables per line. A haiku is written in three lines: five syllables in the first line, seven syllables in the second line, and five syllables in the third line.

Traditionally, a haiku describes one specific moment or place. Though the poem is short, it can express a much larger situation or concept.

Example:

A simple letter,	*5 syllables*
Left alone beside the bed.	*7 syllables*
Fear has left it sealed.	*5 syllables*

- What is your initial feeling from the poem?
- What adjectives would you use to describe it?
- What do you think has happened?

Additional example:

A delicious cake
Is sitting on the table.
Then, Mr. Squiggles.

PART 1 ● Write Your Haiku

Given the structure above, practice writing your own haiku!

PART 2 ● Haiku Factor™

Congratulations – you have been accepted as a top contestant on…Haiku Factor™!

The Rules of the Game: The Haiku Factor™ Host (who looks suspiciously like your instructor) will choose one of the images below. Each person or team will be given a few minutes to write a haiku related to that image. Once everyone has finished, you will present your haiku.

Your haiku will be judged by your peers or the Haiku Factor™ Host! They will give you your score and speak a little bit about how it made them feel.

Your haiku will be judged on the following criteria:

- Creativity – how original and/or interesting
- Style – how well it follows the form and idea of a haiku
- Performance – how well you present your haiku

After several haikus are written, performed, and judged, the person or team with the highest total score is the winner of Haiku Factor™!

Haiku Factor Score Card

(All scores 1 to 5, 5 = best)

Creativity: __ __ __ __ __

Style: __ __ __ __ __

Performance: __ __ __ __ __

Total:

rhyme scheme ***(n.)*:** the pattern of rhyming lines in a poem

LISTENING DIALOGUES SLE 2C

UNIT 1 TRACK 2 and 3

Martha: Thank you for inviting me to your senior art show, Lisa!

Lisa: Thanks for coming, Grandma! I hope you like the work you see.

Martha: Oh my goodness…I love this realistic piece! The detail in the image is absolutely incredible.

Lisa: Do you think so, grandma? I find it a little unimaginative, but his technique is very good.

Martha: Oh, look at this lovely abstract piece! Even though there's not a clear image, the shapes and lines are very bold.

Lisa: I painted that,grandma!

Grandma: It's wonderful, Lisa.

Lisa: Thanks, grandma. Let me show you my favorite image. It's a photograph that my friend Jeff created. Over here! It's really intense the way that the hands are reaching up all covered in paint. What do you think Grandma?

Martha: I kind of don't get it. It seems a bit pretentious.

Lisa: Oh c'mon Grandma! It's so original compared to the other pieces.

UNIT 2 TRACK 4 and 5

Susan: Do you have any plans this afternoon, Richard? I need you to help me in the garden.

Richard: Actually, I'm planning to meet my high school classmate, Stan…

Susan: Oh, that sounds fun!

Richard: Yeah, but there's something about him that always used to bother me, but can't remember what it was.

(Phone Dialing)

Stan: Hello?

Richard: Hi Stan, it's me, Rich! So, what do you want to do?

Stan: Hey Rich! We can do whatever you want to do.

Richard: Why don't we go to a baseball game?

Stan: Whatever you want is fine.

Richard: Okay…baseball it is. When do you want to meet?

Stan: Well…whenever you want is great by me.

Richard: Okay…and where should we meet for lunch? How about Johnny's Pizza?

Stan: We can have lunch wherever you want.

Richard: So…Johnny's, then? At one? Then we can have lunch before the game.

Stan: Whatever works for you. That should be alright.

Richard: Okay then. And why don't I invite some of the other guys?

Stan: Whoever you want!

Richard: Okay, I'll call Jim.

Stan: Jim the plumber, or Jim the bus driver?

Richard: Jim the dancing cowboy.

Stan: Whatever. See ya later.

(Hangs up phone)

Susan: So you've made a plan for later?

Richard: I guess so. I remember what bothered me now…he's the most indecisive person I've ever met! I wish he would express his opinions more.

Susan: What would you like for breakfast Richard?

Richard: Whatever's fine, dear.

UNIT 3 *TRACK 6 and 7*

Jan: Hi Richard. Come on in. My name is Jan Brewer and I'm here to…

Richard: Fire someone, right? I've heard you're an efficiency expert.

Jan: Actually, I'm here to make sure everyone knows what their responsibilities are. Could you tell me what you think your strong points are?

Richard: Well, I'm really good at multi-tasking. I can work on several tasks at the same time.

Jan: I think multi-tasking can lead to projects looking unfinished. It's better to choose what's most important and finish things one at a time.

Richard: Okay. But I'm really good at working until late at night when I need to finish a project.

Jan: It's actually more efficient to work the same number of hours every day. Do you sit at your desk all day or do you move around?

Richard: I do get up and move around frequently. Often I talk with my co-workers about tasks.

Jan: Yes. Your supervisor says that you're often joking and chatting with your co-workers.

Richard: My job is marketing, and I have to get the staff excited. I think that makes me a great team player!

Jan: I can see what you mean. Your co-workers like you a lot. Sometimes it seems, however, that you are slower at completing your side of the project.

Richard: That's just because I'm a perfectionist and I can't complete something until its perfect.

Jan: It's good that you care about your job, but perfectionism can sometimes lead to procrastination.

Richard: I guess I see your point.

UNIT 4 *TRACK 8 and 9*

Susan: Hi, Lisa! How was your day?

Lisa: (sighs) It was TERRIBLE! I just want to crawl into my closet and hide there.

Susan: Oh no! What happened?

Lisa: Well, last year I convinced my friend Tom from high school to go on a date with my friend Tami, who I met in college.

Susan: Is that right? Did they like each other?

Lisa: They really hit it off, and they've been dating for over a year.

Susan: Well, that's wonderful, Lisa. What's the problem?

Lisa: Okay, here's the problem. I was just at the movie theater with Biff, and I saw Tom there with another girl who I didn't recognize!

Susan: Uh oh…

Lisa: What should I do? I've known Tom since high school. I don't want to betray him…

Susan: Certainly not…

Lisa: …but Tami has been my closest friend in university since the first day we met during orientation! I can't just keep a secret from her, but I don't want to end her relationship and hurt her feelings!

Susan: Hmmm…that seems like a real fix, Lisa. You should tell Tami only if you've talked to Tom first.

Lisa: But they seemed awfully friendly. They were sharing popcorn…!

Susan: Even if it looked suspicious, you should still get the facts from Tom. Tell Tami only if you know the facts about the situation.

UNIT 5 *TRACK 10 and 11*

Charles: Thanks for coming cellphone shopping with me Jack. It's been ten over ten years.

Jack: No problem grandpa. Your old phone looks pretty tired. It's definitely time for an upgrade.

Charles: I've only bought two cell phones in twenty years, and I'm proud of that. It looks as if phones have become significantly cheaper. I paid over $300 for my first one back in 1992.

Jack: And because of inflation that phone would cost about $500 in today's prices.

Charles: That's true. Look at this one here. The fuss-free 1000, it's free!

Jack: Well, it's free if you sign a two-year contract. But you have to pay for monthly service for two years.

Charles: What's wrong with that?

Jack: Nothing really. The phone company gets their money back through how much they charge you every month. If you want to go that route, Grandpa, I recommend this one. The I-universe IIIx. It has a touch screen, can surf the web, gives you sports scores, and does a whole lot more for only $299 with a two-year contract.

Charles: But does it make calls?

Jack: Ha. Ha. Sure grandpa. You can even tell it who to call using just your voice!

Charles: And how much is that a month?

Jack: With voice and data it starts at about $70 dollars.

Charles: A month!? I pay twenty now.

Jack: Well, I think if you want to keep your current monthly plan, you could buy the first phone for $129 dollars without contract.

Charles: That sounds like a win.

UNIT 6 TRACK 12 and 13

Charles: Honey, I'm home!

Martha: What perfect timing! Everyone is here, waiting on the pizza. What did you get?

Charles: Well, I couldn't remember exactly what everyone requested, so I just got a meat lover's special. It's got pepperoni, sausage, and bacon. Everyone likes meat.

Martha: Charles...I don't think that everyone likes meat...

Lisa: Oh yum, piz—wait, grandpa, I'm vegetarian!!

Charles: Lisa, I didn't think you were really a vegetarian...I thought that you were just being picky. You ate chicken at dinner last night, remember?

Lisa: Well, I'm trying to be a vegetarian....and meat pizza isn't helping me.

Richard: And I like peppers on the pizza, not pepperoni.

Martha: Charles, you should be eating less meat...this pizza really isn't good for your diet.

Charles: Okay, okay. Maybe I didn't get everyone's absolute favorite pizza, but at least I got a pizza. If you'd like, I'll just take it over to the neighbors' house and eat it with them.

Richard: Well, we didn't say that we won't eat the pizza...

Martha: Yes, the pizza you got isn't ideal, but it's better than nothing.

Lisa: I guess since the pizza is already here, I'll eat meat tonight.

Charles: That's what I thought...

UNIT 7 TRACK 14 and 15

I had the strangest experience last night. I was up in the attic with my cat, Mr. Squiggles, when I discovered a beautiful old mirror. As I got close to it, I felt like I was being watched. I reached out... and my hand went into the mirror! Suddenly, something pulled me in. I remember falling and landing inside a dark cave. There were three doors in the cave. I saw Mr. Squiggles running through the third door.

I climbed what felt like a thousand stairs. When I got to the top of the staircase, I found myself in a large room with piles of papers everywhere. They were exam papers! Hundreds of exam papers!

When I looked up, I saw my boyfriend, Biff! He was sitting in a garden. And...he was pregnant!

I don't know why, but I was suddenly terrified! I quickly climbed a large ladder on the wall. The ladder led me outside into an endless field of roses! I ran through the field and came across a small pond. I dove into the pond and swam down, down, down. At the bottom...at the bottom it was my bed! I wasn't underwater at all! I was in my bedroom. I crawled into bed and had the most wonderful dreams!

UNIT 8 TRACK 16 and 17

Susan: (Crying, distant music in the background) Oh! Umm, hi, Richard. Sorry...

Richard: Ummm...Susan? I know that we don't really know each other that well, but...are you okay?

Susan: Yes, of course. It's prom night!

Richard: I know…everyone says prom night is the best night ever.

Susan: Yeah…I just wish…

Richard: You wish…?

Susan: Well, this is going to sound silly, but I wish I could have been chosen as prom queen! I mean, Kyle's my boyfriend, and he's prom king…I should be queen, not Stephanie! I'm just so disappointed. Plus, I ripped my dress!

Richard: I get it. I mean, I wish I could have been elected prom king!

Susan: Yeah…

Richard: Well, right now, tonight seems like a huge disappointment, but I guess in the future it might just end up as another funny story.

Susan: Haha. Yeah, I guess life isn't about winning a crown at prom, right?

Richard: Right. I guess life is about appreciating what you have. 20 years from now, when I'm a successful world-class heart surgeon…

Susan: …and I own my own restaurant…

Richard: Right, and when you own your own restaurant, then we'll look back on this moment and laugh.

Susan: Yes we will.

Richard: So…do you want to go get some ice cream?

UNIT 9 *TRACK 18 and 19*

Jack: Hey Lisa. I was thinking the other day about that family trip we took.

Lisa: You mean the one when we to see that famous national park?

Jack: Yeah. And it was sooo cold because we expected it to be warm that time of year.

Lisa: Why were you thinking about that?

Jack: Well, I can't remember the name of the guy we met.

Lisa: We met a few people, Jack. Do you mean the guy who we went rafting with?

Jack: No, not that guy. The one we were hiking with when we got chased by that huge angry….

Lisa: Oh yeah! We called him Danimal because he shouted really loud and scared it off.

Jack: Uh-huh. And then we went fishing and made that amazing lunch.

Lisa: I remember that! He had lemons in his backpack! It was really delicious.

Jack: Yeah. That guy. I think he invited me to 'buddy' him on MyFaceWorld.

Lisa: Wow really? What's he up to these days?

Jack: I'm not sure. Let's respond and find out.

UNIT 10 *TRACK 20 and 21*

Lisa: Martha: I'm trying to plan our family outings this year and it's so confusing…

Jack: So long as it's not another family trip. Don't you remember what happened last time?

Martha: Now, now. I think this year, everyone is doing something different with their vacation time. I'm sure nothing will go wrong.

Jack: If you say so. Why is it confusing?

Martha: Well, everyone wants to do something different, and nobody wants to get there the same way.

Jack: What do you mean?

Martha: Well, Susan wants to follow some band around for a few weeks, but the only way to get to each venue is by train.

Jack: Heh, I can't imagine Mom as a roadie. I think she's having a midlife crisis…

Martha: Charles, meanwhile, insists on taking a hot air balloon.

Jack: Really? Sweet! Where is he going on a hot air balloon?

Martha: He plans on landing in some camp site out in the mountains.

Jack: Could be bears…

Martha: At least Lisa's keeping it simple.

Jack: Oh, yeah?

Martha: She wants to help your mother out with her catering business, so she's just going to be taking her bike out for a cooking class.

Jack: Talk about a boring vacation plan. But then again, I guess Dad's stuck going to the office, right?

Martha: Yes, yes. Just got the car fixed and he's got to pay for that by working extra hours.

Jack: Too bad. I was hoping he'd go to the Fun World Theme Park with me.

Martha: Well, you know he gets seasick.

Jack: Oh, yeah, I forgot about that. What about you, grandma?

Martha: Who, me? Ah, I've got a little something planned as well.

Jack: Like what?

Martha: You'd find it quite boring, I'm sure.

Jack: Try me.

Martha: How does jumping out of a plane from 3,000 meters in the air sound?

Jack: Wait, what?!

Martha: Oh, and about Mr. Squiggles…

GLOSSARY SLE 2C

A

Abstract *adjective* not depicting an object, just form — Unit 1
Ambition *noun* desire for success — Unit 7
Anesthesia *idiom* medically induced insensitivity to pain — Unit 4
Anthropology *noun* the study of humankind — Unit 2
Arrogance *noun* behavior that shows you think you are better than others — Unit 9
Associate *verb* mix socially — Unit 9
Attic *noun* open area immediately under the roof of a house — Unit 7
Attire *noun* clothing — Unit 5

B

Back out *phrasal verb* withdraw from a previous commitment — Unit 3
Baggy *adjective* hanging loosely — Unit 5
Bestselling *adjective* bought by many — Unit 1
Between a rock and a hard place *idiom* a difficult situation — Unit 4
Bite off more than you can chew *idiom* to try to do more than you are able to do — Unit 3
Blow it out of proportion *idiom* to overreact to something — Unit 6
Break up *phrasal verb* end a relationship — Unit 1
Bulldozer *noun* a construction vehicle — Unit 1
burglar *noun* someone who enters a building illegally with the intent of stealing something — Unit 9
Buy into *phrasal verb* accept or believe something — Unit 5

C

Call in *phrasal verb* to call and tell work you are not coming — Unit 3
Camper *noun* self-contained traveling home — Unit 1
Capture someone's imagination *idiom* to interest someone in a lasting way — Unit 7
Cast *noun* participants in a performance — Unit 1
Catch a flick *idiom* see a movie in a theater — Unit 1
Chain story *noun* a story written collectively by a group of authors — Unit 9
Check out *phrasal verb* investigate — Unit 1
Chore *noun* household task — Unit 3
Cinematography *noun* technique of photographing motion pictures — Unit 1
Climax *noun* the most important or exciting point — Unit 1
Come up with *phrasal verb* to produce or discover something — Unit 2
Common ground *noun* something mutually agreed upon — Unit 2
Compromise *verb* agreeing to accept less than what was originally wanted — Unit 2
Consideration *noun* careful thought — Unit 2
Conversation piece *idiom* something unusual that provokes conversation — Unit 6
Corner the market *idiom* to become so successful at selling a product that almost no one else sells it. — Unit 5

D

Deep *adjective* intellectually profound Unit 1
DJ *noun* somebody who plays recorded music Unit 1
Dream up *phrasal verb* invent something Unit 7

E

Embellish *verb* to make something sound better or worse than it is Unit 6

F

Fable *noun* story that teaches a lesson Unit 9
Figment of someone's imagination *idiom* something created by the mind that's not really there Unit 7
Fix *noun* a difficult situation Unit 4
Flaky *adjective* an unreliable person Unit 2

G

Game plan *noun* a strategy to achieve a goal Unit 2
Generation *noun* people who were born at approximately the same time period Unit 1
Get into *phrasal verb* appreciate Unit 1
Get it *idiom* understand Unit 1
Get out of *phrasal verb* to avoid doing something Unit 4
Go under *phrasal verb* to bankrupt a business Unit 8
Good/bad taste *idiom* ability to judge Unit 1
Grooming *noun* taking care of personal appearance Unit 7
Guerilla marketing *noun* low cost means used for advertising Unit 5

H

Harsh *adjective* difficult to endure Unit 6
Head in the clouds *idiom* unable to concentrate on reality Unit 7
Heavy responsibility *idiom* very important responsibility Unit 3
Hit it off *phrasal verb* to get along well with someone else Unit 4
Hold someone accountable *idiom* to consider someone responsible Unit 3
Hypnotize *verb* to put someone into a hypnotic state Unit 7
Hypochondriac *noun* someone who is always worried about being sick Unit 7

I

Ice breaker *noun* something used to start a conversation Unit 6
If all else fails *idiom* something you will do if your plans do not succeed Unit 8
Igloo *noun* dome-shaped building built from blocks of snow Unit 1
Indecisive *adjective* unable to make decisions Unit 2

J

Javelina *idiom* a wild pig-like animal, also known as a peccary. Unit 9
Jingle *noun* tune for advertising something Unit 5

K

Key to success *idiom* the way to become successful Unit 8

L

Live out *phrasal* verb to do something previously imagined Unit 7
Lucid *adjective* very clear and real Unit 7
Lukewarm *adjective* just slightly warm Unit 4

M

Measure up *phrasal verb* to be good enough Unit 5
Morale *noun* level of confidence Unit 5

N

Negotiate *verb* to attempt to come to an agreement on something Unit 2
No-win situation *noun* a situation with no good outcome possible Unit 4

O

One-up *phrasal verb* to gain advantage over somebody Unit 10
Original *adjective* creative Unit 1
Own up *phrasal verb* to admit to having done something Unit 3

P

Paralyzed *adjective* unable to move Unit 7
Perk *noun* additional benefit Unit 5
Persistence *noun* the action of doing something without quitting Unit 9
Pick out *phrasal verb* choose something Unit 5
Pick-me-up *idiom* a small something that gives you energy Unit 3
Piece *noun* a single artistic work Unit 1
Placate *verb* to make somebody less angry Unit 4
Plan out *phrasal verb* to make a detailed plan Unit 2
Plot *noun* sequence of events in a novel, play, or movie Unit 1
Pour *verb* to rain very heavily Unit 2
Pretentious *adjective* made to look important Unit 1
Procrastinate *verb* to postpone doing something Unit 3
Psychic *adjective* able to see the future or read people's thoughts Unit 7
Pull something off *phrasal verb* succeed in doing something challenging Unit 8
Pulse *noun* regular beat of blood flow Unit 3

R

Radio spot *noun* a radio advertisement Unit 5
Reap what you sow *idiom/proverb* everything that happens to you is a result of your own actions Unit 9
Rhyme scheme *noun* the pattern of rhyming lines in a poem Unit 10

S

Sequel *noun* continuation of a story Unit 1
Settle on *phrasal verb* to solve a problem Unit 2
Shopping spree *noun* a shopping trip in which a lot of things are purchased Unit 5
Shortcoming *noun* a failure or flaw Unit 5
Simulate *verb* to fake something Unit 6
Slacker *noun* somebody who avoids working Unit 3
Snug *adjective* fitting tightly Unit 5
Spark up *phrasal verb* to start a conversation Unit 6
Stipulation *noun* a demand for something Unit 4
Strike up *phrasal verb* begin a conversation Unit 6
Subordinates *noun* those of lesser rank Unit 9
Subtle *adjective* cleverly indirect Unit 1
Suit *verb* to be the right thing for someone Unit 5
Synopsis *noun* a summary of the plot Unit 1

T

Talk to a brick wall *idiom* the person being spoken to does not listen Unit 6
Talk up *phrasal* verb to praise something in hopes of making it popular Unit 6

V

Vandalize *verb* to destroy another's property without permission Unit 4
Venue *noun* a place where an event is held Unit 4
Viral *adjective* message intended to be spread Unit 5

W

Weigh options *idiom* examine pros and cons Unit 4
Without fail *idiom* something always fails or happens Unit 8
Work through *phrasal verb* to persevere Unit 4